SHANKARA'S UNIVERSAL PHILOSOPHY OF RELIGION

Shankara's Universal Philosophy of Religion

Y. MASIH

Munshiram Manoharlal Publishers Pvt. Ltd.

ISBN 81-215-0007-9
First Published 1987

Published by Munshiram Manoharlal Publishers Pvt. Ltd. Post Box 5715, 54 Rani Jhansi Road, New Delhi-110055 and Printed by Roopabh Printers, 4/115, Vishwas Nagar, Shahdara, Delhi-110032

Contents

Preface **vii**

1

TOOLS OF RELIGIOUS THOUGHT **1**

A. Religion *A Priori* 2
   Christian influence on Hinduism *5;* Indian influence on Christianity *11;* Ontological theory of religion *a priori* *19;* Organismic theory of man and his psyche *22;* Atheism and religion *a priori* *24*

B. Religious Statements Have Nothing to Do with Truth and Falsity 31

C. Religious Statements as Analogical, Pictorial and Symbolical 33
   God and Brahman are unknown and unknowable *33;* *Analogia Entis* *37;* Paul Tillich's theory of symbolism *39;* The theory of symbolism *42;* The 'Truth' of symbolic statements *49;* The religious philosophy of Ludwig Wittgenstein *52;* Paul Tillich, Wittgenstein and Shankara *61*

2

THE RELIGIOUS PHILOSOPHY OF SHANKARA **64**

Introduction *64;* Shankara's monistic philosophy of Brahman *65;* Brahman *66;* The nature of the Jīva *71;* Ahaṁkāra *72;* Jīva and Brahma *74*

Māyāvāda *77*

The origin of Māyāvāda *77;* The nature of Nescience (Ajñāna) *80;* The locus of Māyā *84;* The notion of God *86;* Brahma and Īshvara *88;* Brahma-*jñāna* and theistic proofs *91;* Ontological proof *92;* Cosmological argument *94;* Teleological argument *96;* Liberation (*Mokṣa*) *98;* Karmakāṇḍa and liberation *100;* Worship and liberation *108;* Critical comments with regard to Shankara's theism *111;* Stages of worship *113;* Liberation through *jñāna 115;* Mithyātva (falsity) of Vedānta-Vākyas and release *118;* Mahāvākyas and Brahma-*jñāna 122;* Jīvanmukti *125*

3

THE MODERN RELEVANCE OF SHANKARA **130**

Relativity of deities *133;* Some implications of Shankara's Advaitism *143*

4

THEORETICAL GAINS **146**

Shankara and social change *151*

5

SUMMARY AND CONCLUSION **153**

Bibliography **157**

Index **160**

Preface

The book presents a new interpretation of Shankara's philosophy of religion and gives a defence of Advaitism in the current language of Western philosophy. The book has two parts. Part (I) deals with the framework of religious language and as such contains the theoretical structure of the subject. Part (II) contains the familiar exposition of Shankara's religious thoughts. Against Paul Deussen and Dasgupta the author contends that theism is an integral part of Shankara's religious philosophy. This contention also shows that Shankara was not a Buddhist in disguise but was an Upanishadic thinker. Against the objections of Rāmānuja in the background, the author shows the real nature of the *Mithyātva* of Mahāvākyas in the light of Paul Tillich and Wittgenstein, Samuel Alexander and Russell.

In the first place the author seeks to establish the doctrine of religion *a priori* in the light of parallel development of religious thought both in Christianity and Hinduism. In the opinion of the author the doctrine of religion *a priori* firmly stands supported by ontological and psychological considerations.

Secondly, in the light of Christian, Islamic and Upanishadic thoughts it has been maintained that the ultimate reality is unknown and unknowable. Hence, man impelled by his nature as contained in the doctrine of religion *a priori*, man is thrown into the predicamental situation of trying to know the unknowable. This absurd situation has given rise to the religious philosophies of *analogia entis* (St. Thomas Aquinas), Symbology (Paul Tillich), picture-theories of R.B. Braithwaite and of Wittgenstein.

Shankara, Paul Tillich and Wittgenstein, all contend that there *is* a transcendent reality which underlies all that exists and is talked about, which itself is beyond any empirical language whatsoever. Any attempt at talking about Brahman would trivialize. It and so would falsify It. Hence, one has to maintain silence. Of course

Advaitic philosophers do talk about Brahman with a view to evoking *B-jñāna* in the hearers. But in the end their talk is nothing but nonsense. But it is significant nonsense since it exhibits the secrets contained in the silence of Brahman. This silence has the best prospect of ending all religious disputes and confusion.

The author shows that Shankara's religious philosophy includes all that is abiding in the writings of St. Thomas Aquinas, Paul Tillich and Wittgenstein and in some respects it goes beyond all of them.

Finally, the book shows that the syntax of religious language has to do with the pictures and symbols of the supreme reality, and as such, it should not be assimilated to the language of science and ethics. Proper understanding of the evocative nature of Brahman or God-talk would remove many confusions which beset much of atheistic thinking and the criticism of religion.

Y. Masih

Patna
30 August 1986

1

Tools of Religious Thought

Religion here has been taken to be as an attunement to the supreme Power pervading the whole universe and going beyond it. The *Ṛgvedic* hymn X.90 states that the thousand-eyed Purusha pervades the whole universe and 'fills a space ten fingers wide'. This Power has been beautifully described by Wordsworth in *Lines Written above the Tintern Abbey*:

> And I have felt
> A presence that disturbs me with the joy
> Of elevated thoughts; a sense sublime
> Of something far more deeply interfused,
> Whose dwelling is the light of the setting suns,
> And the round ocean and the living air,
> And the blue sky, and in the mind of man;
> A motion and a spirit, that impels
> All thinking things, all objects of thought,
> And rolls through all things.

The same point has been emphasized by the *Chāndogya Upanishad* (VI. 8-16) by saying that Brahman pervades the sun, moon, water, heat and all things, and yet that Reality is the *Atman* of each individual soul. But in most dramatic way the dynamic presence of the supreme Power can be detected in the evolutionary scheme of matter, life and mind. The emergentists like Ilyod Morgan, Samuel Alexander and others have stated that this power has the two attributes of *conatus* and *nisus*. By virtue of its *conatus* each emergent continues in its own being, and by virtue of its *nisus* it pushes all things towards higher emergence. The important point to emphasize is that the evolutionary *nisus* works in each individual man as is implied by the *Atman*-doctrine of the *Upanishads*. The *nisus* felt in each individual, specially in the prophets, saints and seers, may be interpreted as the call to get attuned to this evolutionary Power. The Delphic oracle or the Upanishadic injunction to know one's *Atman* is a testimony to the view, according to which every man in some degree feels the *nisus* within himself in order to rise above his present self. This 'push and pull' gives rise to a search for an ideal self. And this search may be termed as a religious quest.

It is quite clear from a cursory survey of organic evolution and the history of mankind, that along with progress there has been regress as well. This religious quest for the ideal Self may degenerate into despotism, fanaticism and bloody conquest. Mankind has to guard itself against the abuses of religion.

Again, religion is a social phenomenon, even when a Buddha might be meditating for his Bodhi as a solitary self. Naturally, religion brings about social changes for the weal or woe of the whole mankind. Buddhism, Christianity and Islam stand witness to this fact. Religion as such has to be viewed objectively, and man has to live with it either for his survival or annihilation. Theism, pantheism, polytheism, animism and even all forms of humanism, scientism and materialism have to be viewed as so many varied responses to the same evolutionary *nisus* within each man. Religion here has to be viewed in this wide perspective.

RELIGION A PRIORI

It will perhaps pertain to clearness if the conceptual framework of religious thought be briefly and yet plainly laid out. In doing this, it is supposed here that religion is *a priori*, by which phrase is meant that man knowingly and unknowingly is religious, no matter whatever be his confession on this score. For example, Sigmund Freud declared theistic religion to be an illusion of the human race, and, yet he held firmly to the religion of humanity with its message of universal brotherhood and inner freedom.[1] This is not a solitary instance. At the beginning of *Mahānāṭaka* (or *Hanumānanāṭaka* about AD 850) it is stated:

> "May Hari, Lord of the three Worlds, whom the Shaivas worship as Shiva, the Vedāntins as Brahman, the Buddhists as

[1]Y. Masih, *Freudianism and Religion*, pp. 340-42.

> Buddha, the Logicians, clever in the means of knowledge, as the Creator, devotees of the Jaina doctrine as Arhat, and the Mīmāṃsakas as Karma, ..."[1]

In other words no persons can live without Hari or God. The same doctrine of religion *a priori* has been taught by Udayanācārya about 924 AD in his *Nyāya Kusumāñjali*, chap. I, karika 2:

> "Now with regard to that Being whom all alike worship no matter what end they strive to attain; the followers of the Upanishads as the One by Nature pure and enlightened (*shuddha-buddha-svabhāvaḥ*); the disciple of Kapila as the perfect First Knower (ādividvān), the disciple of Patañjali as the One untouched by hindrance, karma, fruition and impressions of karma, who by assuming a created body revealed by the *Vedas* and who is the giver of the grace; the followers of Mahapashupati as the Independent One, undefiled by actions (even) opposed to the *Veda* or the convention of the world; the Shaivas as Shiva; the Vaiṣṇavas as Purushottama; the Buddhists as the Omniscient; the Digambaras as the One free from obstruction; the Mīmāṃsakas as the One to whom sacrifice is due; the Naiyāyikas as the Being endowed with all attributes which befit him; the Cārvākas as the One whose existence is established by the common consent of the world (lokavyavahārasiddhah . . . . etc.) I ask how can there arise any doubt."

However, the first statement in this connection has been made by the *Ṛgveda:*

> "To what is One, sages give many a title;
> they call it Agni, Yama, Matrishvān" (I. 164.46)

Indian religious philosophers have held fast to it down the ages. Radhakrishnan in our own times has eloquently stated thus:

> "The different religious traditions clothe the One Reality in various images and their visions could embrace and fertilise each other so as to give mankind a many-sided perfection, the

[1]H. Nakamura, *A History of Early Vedānta Philosophy*, p. 355.

> spiritual radiance of Hinduism, the faithful obedience of Judaism, the vision of divine love of Christianity, and the spirit of resignation to the sovereign lord of Islam."[1]

The same teaching of religion *a priori* was taught by Philo of Alexandria (30 BC-AD 50). Philo observed that the world was never bereft of virtuous people, and, he counted Persian Magi and Indian gymnosophists among them. In the same way, Clement of Alexandria (*c.* AD 150-214) sees in the Pagan wise men the same and universal activity of the Logos, as was stated about the Jewish prophets. The ancient wise men include Orpheus, Pythagoras, the Persian Magi, the Druids, the Brahmins and Lord Buddha.

Because Christianity has been a missionary religion and in their zeal many preachers and authors have spoken of other religions in disparaging terms, therefore people ignore the Biblical and other theological statements pertaining to a universal religion and the implicit doctrine of religion *a priori* involved in them. 'He (God) created all the people of the World from one man, Adam, and scattered the nations across the face of the earth' (Acts. 17.26). 'In every nation He has those who worship Him and do good deeds and are acceptable to Him' (Acts. 10; 34-35). According to famous Pauline writing, God has revealed Himself to all people:

> "Ever since God created the world, his invisible qualities .... have been clearly seen; they are perceived in the things that God has made" (*Rom.* 1.20).

Again:

> "To show that you are his sons, God sent the Spirit of his Son into our hearts, the Spirit who cries out 'Father, my Father." (*Gal.* 4.6).

And the same thing has been stated by St. Augustine:

> "Thou has created us for thyself and our heart knows no rest until it may repose in thee."

[1]S. Radhakrishnan, 'Fragments of a Confession' in *The Philosophy of Sarvepalli Radhakrishnan*, p. 79.

Justin, the theologian-martyr expressed his belief in the Universality of Logos (*c.* AD 100-160). Much later Nicholas of Cusa (AD 1453) has uttered the following:[1]

> "God is sought in various ways and called by various names in the various religions, that he has various prophets and teachers in various ages to the various people."

It will not be amiss to note that the ecunemical movement of the Christian churches seeks to unite all spiritually minded people in one world unity of religions. Hence, Anselm of Canterbury (1033-1109) was so convinced of religion *a priori* that he felt that even a fool if he could understand the full connotation of 'God' would not be able to say in his heart 'there is no God'.

Apart from the expressions, both in the East and West, in favour of the doctrine of religion being a universal phenomenon and perhaps 'religion *a priori*' there is the empirical and historical evidence in support of this doctrine.

Christian Influence on Hinduism

With the introduction of the *Gītā* in the West, the European scholars were struck with surprise by finding a close similarity between the teachings of the *Gītā* and the *Bible*. The European Indologists sought therefore to trace Christian influence in the teachings of the *Gītā*. Here three things helped them to draw this conclusion.

1. First, they found the phenomenon of *Kṛṣnajanmāṣṭamī* in which the child Krishna is represented as a suckling at the mother's breast. This representation is said to be a borrowing of 'the Madonna and the child Jesus'. This conclusion is backed by a number of coincidences, namely, Nanda, the foster-father of Krishna had gone to Mathura to pay his taxes (just as Joseph had gone to Bethlehem for census); Krishna was born in a cow-shed (*Gokula* exactly as Jesus was born in a manger); massacre of infants of Mathura by Kamsa (just as was the massacre of infants by Herod); Krishna (like Jesus) had raised the son of a widow from the dead; Kubja annointed Krishna just as Mary had done with precious ointment etc.

[1]Freidrich Heiler, 'How can Christian and Non-Christian Religions Co-operate?' *Hibbert Journal*, 1953-54 p. 109.

From the facts stated above A. Weber concluded that Krishnaism was but plagiarised Christianity. He also held that the monotheism of the *Gītā* and the doctrine of Grace had been borrowed from Christianity.[1] This borrowing was proved from the fact of the presence of Christianity in the South India.

2. There is a tradition that the Apostle Thomas came to India in AD 52. This tradition is not very easy to prove to be historically true. But the fact remains that Indian Christians in South India have remained largely under the Persian Nestorian missionaries. Hence it is conjectured that much of the doctrine of the *Gītā*, concerning monotheism, *bhakti* (faith and *Śraddhā*), the divine grace, has been borrowed from Christianity. In this context, the labours of Lorinser are remarkable. According to Lorinser, there are sixteen passages in the *Gītā* which in meaning and expression agree with the passages of the *Bible*; there are twenty-three passages which have the same expressions but different meanings; and over sixty passages which agree in meaning though differ in expressions.[2] In the same strain George A. Grierson shows that the *Bhaktamālā* consisting of 200 verses only has five very typical characteristic biblical expressions.[3] Further, the cult of *bhakti* has been mentioned in Narayaniya Section of Shānti Parva in the *Mahābhārata*. It is stated here that Nārada, the apostle of *bhakti*, paid a visit to white island (*Shvetadvīpa*) and he describes that white complexioned worshippers are devoted to only one God. Even E.W. Hopkins who does not subscribe to the theory of Christian influence on the *Gītā* states that white-islanders here are foreigners who worship a strange monotheistic God who is not trinitarian.[4]

From the facts stated above, namely, parallel passages both in the *Gītā* and *Bible* (as Lorinser has pointed out), further parallel passages between the *Bhaktamālā* and the *Bible* and the foreign worship implied in the visit of Nārada to *Shvetadvīpa*, George A. Grierson, conjectures that there was the influence of Christianity on the development of Indian *bhakti*. Of course, Grierson

[1] A.Weber, 'On the Krishnajanmasthami', *Indian Antiquary* (*IA*), vol. III, 1874, pp. 21, 47.

[2] 'Traces in the Bhagavadgita of Christian Writings and Ideas', Eng. tr. from the Appendix to Dr. Lorinser's 'Bhagavadgita', 1873.

[3] Geogre A. Grierson, *Journal of Royal Asiatic Society* (*JRAS*), 1907, p. 496.

[4] E.W. Hopkins, *The Religions of India*, p. 432.

admits the origin of *bhakti* to be both indigenous and pre-Christian. But he contends that the subsequent development of modern *bhakti* of India has been influenced by Christianity, as was preached by the Nestorian missionaries.[1]

Grierson's conviction is deepened by the fact that *bhakti* had its origin in the South as the *Bhāgavata Purāṇa* states it.[2] Besides, even the apostles of the northern *bhakti* cult like Rāmānanda, came from the South:[3]

> "All the *bhakti*-sects claim descent from one or other of four chief teachers—Rāmānuja, Viṣṇuswāmi, Madhvācārya, and Nimbaditya. Every one of these belonged to Southern India."[4]

Again, Grierson repeats the same conclusion even after its criticism by J. Kennedy and A.B. Keith in the same volume of *JRAS* 1907, pp. 477-90, (A.B. Keith); 490-92 (J. Kennedy), Grierson writes:

> ". . . . I believe that these (modern forms of *bhakti*) have been in many particular influenced by the cognate doctrines of Nestorians of Southern India. Rāmānuja who was brought up as a Vedāntist, studied, lived . . . within a few miles of the Hindu-Christian shrine of St. Thomas. Similarly, Madhavācharya was born at Udipi, near Kalyāna, where there was an ancient Christian bishopric."[5]

Many other points have been raised, but only a brief reference has been made to them. Are the advocates of Christian influence on Hinduism on sound lines? No. For their views are mere conjectures. So they are easy to refute. Take first the cult of Krishnaism. Against this J. Kennedy advances two very important objections.

(a) *Madonna and Child* representation belongs to the twelfth century, and, the Hindu representation of the suckling divine child

[1]George A. Grierson, 'Modern Hinduism and Its Debt to the Nestorians', *JRAS*, 1907, pp. 315, 494.

[2]*Shrimadbhāgavata Mahāpurāṇa*, ch. I, p. 47.

[3]G.A. Grierson, *JRAS*, 1907, p. 501.

[4]Ibid., p. 502.

[5]G.A. Grierson, 'The Narayaniya and Bhagavatas', *IA*, 1908, p. 250n.

is much earlier in the paintings of Elura.[1] In this connection, M. Foucher has shown that the Devaki-putra of *Chāndogya Upanishad*, III.17.6 worshipped on the occasion of *Kṛṣḥnajanmāṣṭamī* really belongs to Buddhist Madonna Hariti of Mahāyāna iconography.[2] A. Barth too relates Devaki and Krishna child with Māyādevi and child Siddārtha.[3] A. Barth, taking many other points into account concludes that the traces of Christian influence on the myth of Krishna and His worship are absolutely improbable.[4]

(b) J. Kennedy admits that there were small Christian communities in the South, but it was impossible for them 'to have exercised any considerable influence on the evolution of Northern Hinduism'.[5]

(c) H.G. Rawlinson[6] observes that the parallels between the life stories of Lord Krishna and Jesus 'are vague and unsatisfactory':

> "Still less convincing are the parallels between the *Gospels* and the *Bhagavadgītā* collected with such industry by Lorinser."

Further, the description of *Shvetadvīpa* or white island is purely poetical and 'there is no reason to suppose that any reference to Christianity is intended in the remotest fashion.'

The conclusion is that in India and in the West parallel coincidences took place with regard to Krishnaism and Christianity. The purpose here is not to get the problem settled, but to show that even astounding coincidences in religious stories and worship may take place amongst people, untouched by mutual influences.[7] This conclusion will support the thesis that religion is *a priori*, and the people far apart may come to reach very similar development on account of similar spiritual hunger and proclivities. This conclusion is supported by a consideration of the second point with regard to the borrowings in the *Gītā* concerning monotheistic worship, *bhakti* (faith) and the divine grace.

[1]J. Kennedy, 'Krishna, Christianity and the Gurjarars', *JRAS*, 1907, pp. 483-84.

[2]Kalidas Nag, *Greater India*, pp. 243-44.

[3]A. Barth, *Religions of India*, p. 167n.

[4]Ibid., p. 224.

[5]J. Kennedy, *JRAS*, 1907, p. 957.

[6]H.G. Rawlinson, *Intercourse Between India and the Western World*, pp. 177-78.

[7]In my opinion, the problem is still open and requires very careful research.

In my opinion, H.G. Rawlinson in a cavalier fashion has brushed aside the parallel passages between the *Gītā* and the *Bible*, and likewise perhaps, he would also brush aside the five typical Christian teachings mentioned in the *Bhaktamālā* and the *Bible*, pointed out by George A. Grierson. Both A. Barth and A.B. Keith raise one important objection with regard to the kind of *bhakti* in the *Gītā* and Christianity. According to them, the doctrine of faith in Christianity goes with the doctrine of atonement. But the *bhakti* of the *Gītā* is quite free from the doctrine of atonement. Hence, *bhakti* of the *Gītā* is an indigenous development with its origin in the *Vedas* and the *Upanishads*.[1]

Hence, given the rise of monotheism through the hymns of *Prajāpati*, *Hiraṇyagarbha* and so on, the flowering of *bhakti* follows as a natural development in Hinduism. Of course, Grierson, following R. Garbe admits the fact of indigenous origin of *bhakti* in India, but he holds that Krishnaic *bhakti* of the *Gītā* developed under the influence of Christianity.

Grierson's strong point was that *bhakti* arose in the South and all the important teachers of *bhakti* had their linkage with the South. Further there were the Nestorian Christians in the South. Hence, *bhakti* cult developed under the influence of Christianity. In my opinion, neither A.B. Keith nor J. Kennedy has responded to this challenge of Grierson. But should we really trace the development of *bhakti* to the Christian influence?

Some of the most important religious cults of India like Jainism, Buddhism and even much of the Upanishadic teaching are non-Brahminical. Could this thirst for spiritual yearning be held back from the non-Aryans, called Shudras? When the Shudras (which simply mean non-Brahmins in the South) were denied the rights of Vedic learning and rituals, then they took to *bhakti*, pertaining either to Shiva or Viṣṇu. This is specially true of the Ālvārs, whose philosophy on devotion was taken over and systematised by Rāmānuja. Thus, K.R. Subramaniam writes:

> "It is peculiar that some of the earliest saints are drawn from the lower classes and the majority of those whom Sundara

[1]'Bhakti' has been traced to the *Ṛgveda*, 1.71.7; II.26.3; VI.1.5,13; VI.47.1; X.51.32; X.149.4; and the hymn of faith X.151. The following references have been made to the *Upanishad Bṛhadāraṇyaka*, 1.4.15; II.4.5; *Chāndogya*, VII.26.2; *Mund.*, 1.28; *Kath.*, II.23; *Shvet.*, III.8; VI.18.

> thought to include in his list of devotees are also from the same orders . . . it indicates at least that *bhakti* in the Tamil land was at first popular outside the Brahmanical caste."[1]

The notion of equality and devotion is peculiar to the South, which is opposed to Brahminical doctrine of caste. This explanation in terms of the non-Brahminical origin of *bhakti* is fairly intelligible. Hence it is not necessary to trace the Christian influence on the development of *bhakti* in the South, as Grierson had imagined. It is also noteworthy that the South was also rich in producing some of the remarkable teachers of Mahāyāna Buddhism, which was also opposed to caste.

But the most important point in this regard either in favour or against Christian influence depends on the time of the *Gītā* itself. This is a ticklish problem and even now it is difficult to ascertain the date of the *Gītā* in its present form. But if Krishnaism is the same as *Bhagavata bhakti* or Vasudevism, then it has to be treated as pre-Christian on the following grounds:

1. *Pāṇini's Vasudeva*—Sūtra IV.3.98. The use of 'Vasudevaka' shows that it refers to Vasudeva as a person who is the object of *bhakti*. Pāṇini is supposed to have lived about 350 BC.
2. Patañjali in his *Mahābhāṣya* (about 150 BC) speaks of Vasudeva as the worshipful one.
3. Two inscriptions dated *c*. 150 BC and 100 BC speak of Vasudeva as the god of gods, showing the pre-Christian worship of Vasudeva.
4. Then there is the Greek report of Indian worship by Megasthenes who was a Greek ambassador in the reign of Chandragupta (302-288 BC). This report usually has been interpreted as the worship of Krishna and Shiva, as the then popular form of religion in India.

Of course, none of the points stated above are free from controversies.[2] But the general impression among the Indologists is that the cult of Krishnaism is pre-Christian. Besides, talking about *bhakti*, A.B. Keith observes that *bhakti* from the first is the

[1]K.R. Subramaniam, *The Origin of Śaivism and Its History in the Tamil Land*, p. 63.

[2]The book *Megasthenes and Indian Religion* by Allan Dahlquist, has raised powerful controversies with regard to the points in favour of pre-Christian origin of Krishnaism.

characteristic of Rāma worship, which if not anterior to Christian era, is certainly prior to the period in which Christian influence could have been possible on the Indian thought.[1]

If the *Gītā* in the present form, at least in the form in which *bhakti* was the dominant trend of the *Gītā* be pre-Christian, then any talk of Christian influence on the *Gītā* is out of court. Now K.T. Telang, in the Introduction to the *Bhagavadgītā*, first published in 1882, shows that the *Gītā* in the present form is pre-Christian. Hence, there can be no possibility of Christian influence on the *Gītā*. Similarly, E.W. Hopkins states that in spite of close resemblance to the Christian religion, the *Gītā* is really a later *Upanishad*, having kinship with *Kathopanishad*.[2] As the *Upanishads* in general, are pre-Christian, so the *Gītā* too is pre-Christian. Hence, there can be no Christian influence on the *Gītā*.

G.S. Khair, *Quest for the Original Gītā*, J.E. Turner, *The Original Gītā* and others will dispute the view of K.T. Telang. But without raising any further controversies, the conclusion is that the *bhakti* cult of the *Gītā*, its monotheism and the doctrine of grace have all developed indigenously without any foreign influence of the West. This shows that men are but men, and, given the same climate of thought they reach the same conclusion about God, because God has not left Himself without a witness in all ages and races of men. This shows that religion is as natural in man as breathing is, once a man is roused from his unconcerned slumber pertaining to what concerns him absolutely.

Considering that the *Gītā* is pre-Christian and certainly the missionary religion of Buddhism is pre-Christian, cannot many of the Biblical statements, Christian beliefs and practices be due to Indian influence.

Indian Influence on Christianity

We have already mentioned that Philo (30 BC-AD 50) and Clement of Alexandria (*c.* AD 150-214) regard Indian sages to be the recipient of divine revelation and Clement names "Brahmins" and "Buddha", specifically. Hence, the influence of the missionary religion of Buddhism, and, possibly of Jainism and Vasudevism cannot by discounted. It is a fact that Greek rulers did embrace

[1]A.B. Keith, *JRAS*, 1907, p. 491.
[2]E.W. Hopkins, *The Religions of India*, p. 389.

Buddhism and Vasudevism, and, Buddhism found its way up to Asia Minor.

In the early development of Christianity, Manichaenism and Gnosticism played the part of heresies, and, both of them have been traced to Indian influence:

> "The debt of Neo-Platonism to Oriental sources is indisputable, and when we observe the extent of the knowledge about Eastern beliefs exhibited, not only by Origen, but by orthodox writers like Clement and St. Jerome, we cannot help wondering whether Christianity does not owe some of its developments . . . . monasticism and relic worship, for instance, ... to Buddhist influence".[1]

Here one need not be reminded of the fact that in Buddhism monks alone were deemed fit for Nirvana, and, they lived in monasteries where all things were held in common, even the begging bowls and umbrellas. Each monk had to take the vows of celibacy, poverty and moral discipline.

These are the very vows which even now the Roman Catholic priests have to take, and, no doubt the monasticism in Christianity was influenced by Buddhism. Similarly, the Roman Catholic Christians have to confess their sins before the priest for their forgiveness through priestly intercession. However, the practice of *Uposhatha* (confession) is very old in Buddhism.[2] In the assembly of monks, one monk will charge the guilty monk of his acts of omission and commission, and, the guilty one had to confess before the whole assembly. This rite of confession was deemed to be a very great purificatory act. Hence, it appears that the rite of confession in Christianity is indebted to Buddhism.

It is strange, however to note that H.G. Rawlinson suggests that the Christian monasticism was more due to the Jewish monastic order of the Essenes of the Dead Sea.[3] But from where the Essene sect could have been influenced? Philo of Alexandria observes that the Essenes did not treasure silver and gold, nor did they acquire any property or house or anything of this sort. But they deposited

[1]H.G. Rawlinson, *Intercourse Between India and the Western World*, p. 138.

[2]*Vishuddhi Mārga*; also Acharya Narendradeva, *Bauddha-Dharma-Darshan*, p. 7.

[3]H.G. Rawlinson, *India and the West*, p.176.

everything they owned in public together and the benefit of which was enjoyed by the inmates of the Essene order. The early Christians too, as has been mentioned in the Biblical book of Acts, chapters IV and V appear to have been influenced by the Essenes. James Moffath observes that the Essenes were influenced by Pythagoreanism and Orphism. But he also adds that Buddhistic tendencies probably shaped certain tendencies in Essenism.[1] Therefore, Christian monasticism is indirectly indebted to Buddhism, for certainly the Essene monasticism has a great many features in common with Buddhism.

Again, relic worship (in the form of several days in honour of saints in Roman Catholic calendars[2]) and the use of church-bells and rosary have been traced to Indian influence.[3] But relic worship of the Buddhists in the form of stupas is an important element in the evolution of crucifix. The stupa is really a symbol of phallius worship. John Irwin, a British art historian observes that early Christian cult crosses were not crucifixes but pillars. The only kind of cross associated with them was a small wheel-cross on the top, a sun-symbol like the early Indian 'cakra'.[4] Here John Irwin should have also noted that 'cakra' was an important symbol of Buddhist dharma-cakra (circle). Hence, the Buddhist relic worship might have helped the evolution of crucifix.

There is, again, a close resemblance between Lord Buddha and Jesus Christ. Both of them leave home about the same age of 29-30. Both were tempted before they overcame their temptations. Lord Buddha was variously tempted by Māra before he got his enlightenment (*bodhi*), and Jesus Christ too was tempted by the Devil. Even some of the Biblical utterances can be directly traced to the Buddhist influence It is a well-known fact that in one of the *Jātaka* stories Lord Buddha as a Bodhisattva teaches that *hiṃsā* (violence) cannot be conquered except through non-violence and love. And this is the typical Christian teaching (Mt. v, 38-42; Luke VI.29-30). In the same way, Lord Buddha is spoken of as 'Light made manifest in the World'. In a fragment of a drama, perhaps by Ashvaghosa (about first century AD), a dialogue is presented between Dhriti,

[1]James Moffath, 'Essenes', *ERE*, vol. 5, p. 401.

[2]H.G. Rawlinson, *India and the West*, pp. 138, 176.

[3]A. Barth, *The Religions of India*, p. 224.

[4]A staff reporter, 'Importance of Pillar, Cross in World-Cults', *The Times of India*, dated 11 Feb. 1979, p. 4.

Kirti and Buddhi. It is stated there that Buddha as 'the dharma in the form of a man is the light manifest in the world'.[1] Again, there occurs a statement in the *Buddha-caritra* which is a famous utterance attributed to Jesus:

> "Better far with red-hot iron pins bore out both your eyes than encourage in yourself lustful thoughts, or look upon a woman's form with such desires."[2]

The Biblical statement is:

> "So if your right eye causes you to sin, take it out and throw it away! It is much better for you to lose a part of your body than to have your whole body thrown into hell. If your right hand causes you to sin, cut it off and throw it away! It is much better for you to lose one of your limbs than for your whole body to go to hell" (Mt. V: 29-30).

Both of the Biblical utterances have been quoted in *Bhaktamālā*.[3]

Further, H.G. Rawlinson states that Archelaus of Carrha (AD 278) and St. Jerome (AD 340) both mention Lord Buddha by name and narrate the story of his virgin birth. He continues:

> "The Buddha story became gradually known in the West, until by a coincidence hardly to be paralleled in literature, it was narrated in the eighth century AD by John of Damascus as the life of a Christian saint. Under the guise of Saint Josaphat, Gautama the Bodhisattva found his way into the Christian Church, and was included in the Martyrology of Gregory XIII (1582)."[4]

Similarly, gnosticism has greatly influenced Christianity, and, St. John is permeated with gnostic teaching. The Biblical statement is,

[1]Kalidas Nag, *Greater India*, pp. 250-59. One of the scenes of this fragmentary drama is reproduced in Ashvaghosa's *Buddha-caritra*.

[2]'A Life of Buddha', *SBE*, XIX, verses 1862, 1763.

[3]G.A. Grierson, 'Modern Hinduism and Its Debt to the Nestorians', *JRAS*, 1907, p. 496.

[4]H.G. Rawlinson, *India and the West*, p. 142, where Rawlinson makes reference to J.W. McCrindle, *Ancient India*, p. 184, and Max Müller, *Selected Essays*, I, p. 500.

'If ye know the truth, the truth shall make you free'. Again, when the Helper in the form of Holy Spirit comes, then He will reveal the truth about God (St. Jn. 14. 16-17; 18:37). What is gnosticism? First, it is the same Saṃskṛta root *jña* from which *gnosticism* in Greek language emerges. Quoting Theodorus, Clement of Alexandria describes gnosis as:

> "the knowledge of who we were, what we have become, where we were, into what place we have been thrown; wither we are hastening, whence we are redeemed; what is birth, what is rebirth."[1]

The question is certainly Upanishadic and it has been beautifully put much later by Shankara (AD 788-820):

> 'who you are, who I am, whence we are, who my mother is and who my father is.'[2]

Of course, the starting point of both Eastern and Western enquiry emphasised the need for 'Self-knowledge'. But like the *Upanishad*, gnosticism states that *jñāna* can be attained only through mystical enlightenment, 'an immediate vision of truth', 'insight into the mind of God, even to a participation in the Divine nature'. It also teaches the doctrine of redemption which means a deliverance from the material world, which is regarded as 'intrinsically evil', blended with the further idea of escape into a world of freedom, or a return to the original place in heaven.[3]

Certainly Clement of Alexandria whose death took place between AD 214 and 220 knew accurately about transmigration. But many Indologists have traced the doctrine of gnosticism to Persian and Greek sources. It was J. Kennedy who has traced Indian influence in Christian gnosticism. J. Kennedy with his immense knowledge of the then archaeology writes:

> "If Buddhism was to influence Christianity, Gnosticism might

[1]E.F. Scott, 'Gnosticism', *ERE*, vol. 6, p. 231, *Chāndogya*, VIII.7-12; VI.8.7; *Bṛhadāraṇyaka*, II, 4.6 etc.

[2]*Charpatapanjarika-Stotram*, verse II.

[3]E.F. Scott, *ERE*, vol. 6, pp. 231-32, 234-35.

> be supposed to furnish the most likely channel. Gnosticism was anterior to Christianity, and was open to Indian influence."[1]

He also contends that Gnosticism is not pure Hellenism, as some say; it is rather pure Orientalism in a Hellenic mask. This Buddhist gnosticism, according to J. Kennedy, permeated into Christianity through Basilides:

> "If I discover Buddhist pessimism and transmigration in Clement, Buddhist metaphysics in Hippolytus, and Buddhist psychology in both, it is evident that both are describing a single system . . . . the system of the master (Basilides)."[2]

According to J. Kennedy, Basilides was a true Christian and he adapted Buddhist philosophy, metaphysics and psychology for establishing a Christian theology. If the contention of J. Kennedy be accepted, then one has to admit Buddhist influence on Christian theology. Then one finds an echo of both the doctrines of transmigration and incarnation in the Gospels. Take the question of transmigration. A man born blind was brought before Jesus. His disciples asked:

> 'Teacher, whose sin caused him to be born blind? Was it his own or his parents' sin?, (Jn. 9.2).

Jesus did not answer this question directly, but parried it:

> "His blindness has nothing to do with his sins or his parents' sins. He is blind so that God's power might be seen at work in Him" (Jn. 9.3).

That is, even at the time of Jesus, the Jewish people did entertain the thought of transmigration. This might be due to the Pythagorean influence or Buddhist. The question remains open.

There is also a reference about reincarnation in the Gospels. According to Mathew 11.14 John the Baptist was Elijah reborn.

[1]John Kennedy, 'Buddhist Gnosticism, the System of Basilides', *JRAS*, 1902, p. 379.

[2]Ibid., pp. 387-88.

More elaborately:

> "Then the disciples asked Jesus, 'why do the teachers of the Law say that Elijah has to come first?' 'Elijah is indeed coming first', answered Jesus, 'and he will get everything ready. But I tell you that Elijah has already come and people did not recognise him, but treated him just as they pleased. In the same way they will also ill-treat the Son of Man'. Then the disciples understood that he was talking to them about John the Baptist" (*Mt.* 17. 10-13).

We have already referred to Clement's reference to 'birth and rebirth' in connection with Gnosticism. Thus, the doctrine of rebirth was prevalent at the time of the writings of the Gospel. It is difficult to say how much of it was Pythagorean or Buddhist.

In modern times Indian Christians like Brahmabandhab have adopted Vedāntic theology and Chenchiah has used Aurobindo's doctrine of super-mind through Yoga. But Paul Tillich too has adopted Advaitic thinking and talks of 'God beyond God', which is another name of *Brahman*. But our context is not modern, but ancient Christianity. Can we say that the origin of Christian thought and practice owes anything to Indian influence?

We have adduced the evidence of Indian influence on Christianity, but certainly, beyond the kind of evidence already mentioned there is no direct documentary and archaeological data to support the thesis of Indian influence on Christianity. K.M. Panikkar states that there is no evidence to substantiate the view that Essene creed and gnosticism were influenced by India.[1]

Again, H.G. Rawlinson states that India remained uninfluenced by Hellenism and Persian thought:

> "Hellenism, which affected profoundly the whole of Western Asia and even Egypt, stopped short at the Hindu Kush, in spite of the presence of a Greek *rāni* at Pataliputra and of the close and friendly relations existing between the Mauryas and their brother monarchs of Syria and Egypt. Chandragupta, who had spent his early days as an exile in the Punjab, where Persian civilization had taken a stronghold on the country,

[1]K.M. Panikkar, *Studies in Indian History*, pp. 2-3.

> was imbued with Persian ideas. Of Greek culture he and his successors exhibit hardly a trace."[1]

And if we maintain that Christianity too remained untouched by Indian thought, then we have to maintain that the resemblances between Christianity, the *Gītā* and Rāmānuja's theism are paralleled coincidences and can be attributed to the broad similarities in the human mind itself. This will lend support to the doctrine of religion *a priori*. It is remarkable that Pythagoreanism . . . . with its doctrine of transmigration and vegetarianism originated in the West independently of the Indian influence and about the same time.

This doctrine of 'religion *a priori*', will get wide support if we study the archaeology of early phase of religion in terms of manaism, animism and totemism. These archaic forms of early religions were found in almost all the races of the world. What else would support the doctrine of religion *a priori* more powerfully?

This contention shows that human nature is the same in all climes and works in almost in the same identical manner in its different stages of growth.[2] This is quite clear from a study of primitive religions scattered about the whole world. Thus, Westropp and Wake observe:

> ". . . . the human nature is so constituted that the same objects and the same operations of nature will suggest like ideas in the minds of men of all races, however widely apart."[3]

For example, the worship of Baal or goddess Asherah amongst the Jews and the worship of Shiva *liṅgam* in India are such parallel developments. The serpent as the phallic symbol is found in the story of Adam and Eve; the serpent was also hung up from the pole in the wilderness during the sojourn of the Jews for the promised land; and the veneration of pillars (as another phallic symbol) from the time of Jacob onwards. Bulls and rams were also sacrificed by the Jews and even worshipped as fertility rites.

It is also surprising that the imagery of Christ as the husband of the church as his spouse is paralleled in the *bhakti* cult of the Ālvars.

[1]H.G. Rawlinson, *India and the West*, p. 161.
[2]H.M. Westropp, and Staniland Wake, *Ancient Symbol Worship*, pp. 23, 89.
[3]Ibid., p. 24.

Thus, we can conclude that religion is deep-rooted in man and finds its fulfilment in various forms in all ages. Man can hardly live without some form of worship or commitment to values. Why ?

Religion lies in getting attuned to whatever may be deemed as the ultimate reality which is in the sun, moon and rolls through all things. The presence of this ultimate reality is easily detected in the evolutionary scheme of matter, life and mind. Even mind shows progress from the non-moral state to a state of morality, leading to some kind of worship and commitment to values. Since the evolution of man there does not appear the emergence of any higher biological creature. But certainly man has been evolving in his thought-aspect and about his ideal nature. Hence, the *nisus* of the evolutionary scheme, impelling the highest evolute so far, has become articulate in man. This is not a vain fiction, since man contains within himself the vestiges of previous history of evolution. He is the physico-chemical organism imbued with the collective memory of the whole human race. His ideals and values seem to anticipate what man is going to be. Hence, both history and prophecy are included in what man is, as was taught by Pringle-Pattison. His prophecy in terms of his hopes and fears betrays the presence of the impingement of the supreme reality which impels him to raise above his present state of affairs. Naturally each man feels the *conatus* and *nisus* of the evolutionary course of that which sweeps across all the events of this universe. It is any wonder that man with the evolutionary *nisus* within him for something still higher cannot live without some form of religion?

Ontological Theory of Religion a priori

Of course, ontological theory as *a priori* and in their present temper of philosophising it is not given much weight. But this much is clear from the ontological statements concerning the immortality and eternality of the Soul, both in the East and West that they pertain to religion *a priori* from their belief in the pristine existence of souls in their purity and glory.

Plato, specially in *Phaedo* (72 *c*-76) and *Phaedrus* (248-50) speaks of the eternity, immortality and pristine purity of the Soul.[1] He also talks of the transmigration of souls. But the important thing

[1]*Plato*, edited E. Hamilton and H. Cairns, *Bollingen Series*, LXXI, Princeton, 1971.

is that for Plato all true knowledge is recollection. It is this reminiscence of the pristine glory of the soul which makes man pursue what is good, true and beautiful, in other words, the pursuit of a virtuous or religious experience. The same point is made out in Indian philosophy.

Indian philosophy of Jainism, Sāṃkhya-Yoga and to some extent Nyāya and Rāmānuja's Viśiṣṭādvaitism admits the pristine existence of souls. Either through ignorance of Karman (Jainism, Rāmānuja) the soul falls into the miserable existence of earthly life. This kind of miserable existence continues in the chain of rebirths till the right knowledge dawns. But why should one hanker after right knowledge for one's final release? Well, it is the very nature of each soul in bondage to regain its pristine glory. Hence, each soul so made that it will strive for its release. Thus, religious pursuit is the nature of each man born into the world. In Rāmānuja's system there is an additional reason. Each man is a part of God's body, wholly dependent on Ishvara, and, Ishvara is the indwelling spirit of the world and jīvas. It is this indwelling spirit, which at the right moment, impels man to regain his former pristine state of dependence on and closeness with the Lord, characterized by a great deal of spiritual excellence and power.

Thus, according to Indian thought predominantly there is an urge within man to be religious. He may fall into lowly forms of worship, like the worship of demons, or he may rise into the higher forms of spiritual attainment. Hence, Indian thought largely teaches the doctrine of religion *a priori*.

In our own day, it was Paul Tillich (1886-1966) who has most powerfully advanced the doctrine of religion *a priori*. In the concluding lines of *Dynamics of Faith*, Paul Tillich writes:

> ". . . . faith is not a phenomenon besides others, but the central phenomenon in man's personal life, manifest and hidden at the same time. It is religious and transcends religion, it is universal and concrete, it is infinitely variable and always the same. Faith is an essential possibility of man, and therefore its existence is necessary and universal."

Faith depends on the presence of an ultimate concern of man for the ultimate.[1]

[1]Paul Tillich, *Dynamics of Faith*, pp. 45, 50, 75, 77, 101, 106, 114.

"The ultimate concern is unconditional, independent of any conditions of character, desire or circumstance. The unconditional concern is total; no part of ourselves or of our world is excluded from it; there is no 'place' to flee from it."[1]

Then again Paul Tillich writes:

"The fundamental symbol of our ultimate concern is God. It is always present in any act of faith, even if the act of faith includes the denial of God, where there is ultimate concern, God can be denied only in the name of God. One God can deny the other one. Ultimate concern cannot deny its own character as ultimate."[2]

Of course, Tillich grants the possibility of remaining unconcerned about one's own ultimate concern,[3] even though it is questionable for Tillich for one to be without one's concern. The reason for saying this is that, according to Tillich, man is always placed in his paradoxical and existential situation of anxieties, insecurities, estrangements and other ambiguous conditions of life. On the whole, 'A God disappears; divinity remains'.[4] Again, a symbol and myth are the expressions of one's faith:

"One can replace one myth by another, but one cannot remove the myth from man's spiritual life."[5]

Even humanism which ostensibly denies religion is also a form of faith, according to Tillich:

". . . . if faith is understood as the state of being ultimately concerned about the ultimate, humanism implies faith. Humanism is the attitude which makes man the measure of his own spiritual life . . . . For humanism the divine is manifest in the human; the ultimate concern of man is man."[6]

[1]Paul Tillich, *Systematic Theology*, vol. I, p. 12, also see p. 13.
[2]Paul Tillich, *Dynamics of Faith*, p. 45.
[3]Ibid., pp. 45-46.
[4]Ibid., p. 18.
[5]Ibid., p. 50.
[6]Ibid., pp. 62-63.

The ontological reason for Tillich is that man is infinitely concerned about Being-itself to which he belongs, from which he has been estranged. Here one finds the echo of Augustine and St. Paul, according to whom one cannot find rest unless one finds rest in God. Thus Tillich writes:

> "Man is totally concerned about the totality which is his true being and which is disrupted in time and space. Man is unconditionally concerned in time and space. Man is unconditionally concerned about that which conditions his being beyond all the conditions in him and around him."[1] Here is the echo of Shankara's *avacchedavāda*.

Thus, Tillich subscribes to the doctrine of religion *a priori*.

Organismic Theory of Man and His Psyche

It was Aristotle who first advanced the theory of *horme* by virtue of which every organism tends to become a whole and complete. Later on, Spinoza declared that there is a central drive or conatus . . . . in each organism which preserves it in its own being. Without elaborating the concept of 'holism' it can be said that Samuel Alexander, Field Marshall J.C. Smuts, A.N. Whitehead, Paul Tillich have all maintained an organismic theory in their philosophy. Now keeping to the level of science, we can say that it was Hans Adolf Eduard Driesch (1867-1940) who emphasized the working of a holistic drive in each organism. This drive is specially noticeable in an embryo which takes the form of its species and because of this drive tries to repair any injury done to the embryo in the process of its development. Later on Lashley working on the injury of the brain in the study of learning process emphasized the holistic process of the brain, that is, the remaining part of the brain after the lesion of some of its parts, takes over the function of the parts removed from the brain.

But the doctrine of holism becomes interesting when it is applied to the study of the total personality. It was indirectly hinted at by S. Freud when he stated that each organism tends to maintain an

[1]Paul Tillich, *Systematic Theology*, vol. I, p. 14.

equilibrium of certain potentials.[1] Again, C.G. Jung has always maintained that there is a holistic tendency in each individual by virtue of which after making successful adaptation to the outer world, each individual tries to realise the full potentialities of his inner psyche in the second half of his life. He mentions the four stages of Shadow, Anima-animus, Mana personalities and Mandala experience. The whole process of individuation described by Jung, in general outline is an echo of the Advaitic and Buddhistic teaching of reaching the ultimate goal of Brahman and nirvana respectively.

Very interestingly the organismic theory has been advanced in the building of human personality according to Kurt Goldstein Andras Angyal, Abraham Maslow, Prescott Lecky, Carl Rogers and others. Like Jung, Goldstein emphasizes the adjustive processes within the organism itself in the task of self-actualization. This process is known as *autonomy*. Apart from autonomy, there is the process of *homonomy* by virtue of which an individual expands and enriches his personality by appropriating and incorporating things and values from the environment. At the psychological level the individual forms an image of his whole personality which, according to Andras Angyal may be termed as his 'Symbolic Self'. It is this symbolic self which gives rise to the formation of one's deity or the notion of one's highest self either as Brahman or Nirvana.

As a psychological organism, an individual gets conscious of his drive to become his symbolic self, which embodies the whole meaning of life, in relation to his total lived sphere of his environment, as Lewin has termed it. Thus the centring or central driving force within the individual to become his own Symbolic Self makes an individual transcend his own narrow individuality to become his spiritual self. It is this drive which is at the basis of religion *a priori*. A theist would say that God Himself has left His Seal on each individual by virtue of which he would not find rest, except when he finds his rest in God. Others tend to realise their spiritual

[1]*Beyond the Pleasure Principle*, pp. 50-51 of course, Freud was not without religion. He entertained Jewish messianic hope of a millennium in *Future of an Illusion*, pp. 85-86, 93. Then again, religion of Stoic resignation or Buddhist *Upeksa* (*Letters of Sigmund Freud*, p. 276) coupled with the ideals of brotherly love, inner freedom and truth (Erich Fromm, *Psychoanalysis and Religion*, p. 21) was taught by Freud. Hence, even Freud was not without a religion.

'whole' in other than theistic ways. But no man can live without some religion.

Objectors and scoffers would say that it is a worthless attempt to make people religious by defining it. But our attempt has been made as a result of a consensus on this point by appealing to the views, ancient and modern, empirical, historical and psychological. After all philosophy is concerned with the vision of the whole reality, specially with regard to the ultimate human destiny. No views can be final. First, because we are all finite. Secondly, we are still in the midst of evolution, the beginning and end of which are shrouded in the cloud of unknowing. But decision has to be made with all the resources at our disposal. In the 'yah' and 'nay' of religious thought and its many and varied promptings, a philosopher discovers his own depth, and, in this discovery or self-disclosure one finds his own authentic self which is the prize of human living.

But atheism has been a conspicuous feature of contemporary philosophy and even of Christian theology, either directly (of Christian priests involved in the movement of 'God is dead') or indirectly (Paul Tillich's, R. Bultmann's and D. Bonhoeffer's) as Bishop Robinson sees in *Honest to God*. Hence, we cannot so easily brush aside a consideration of atheism as a possible objection to the doctrine of religion *a priori*.

Atheism and Religion a priori

About fifty years ago, largely under the influence of Wittgenstein's *Logico-philosophicus Tractatus*, analytic philosophy has made one of the most drastic attack on theism. J.N. Findlay who is not himself an atheist has shown in *Ontological Atheism* that God-talk is absurd and self-contradictory. The reason? Christian theism, according to him, is based on the notion of a *necessary Being*. But if God is necessary, then it is a matter of an analytic proposition concerned with the consistent use of terms in their stipulated definition. Hence, God is not a being or fact. If, on the other hand, God is a *being* or *fact*, then only a synthetic proposition is possible, not a necessary statement. Hence, any talk about God as a *necessary Being* makes a self-contradictory statement, either that God is both necessary and synthetic, or synthetic and necessary.

A. Flew extended this atheistic attack still deeper. According to him, God-talk is an assertion and therefore as an assertion it must be falsifiable. But God-talk is not falsifiable, because of the shifting grounds of theistic language or commitment of a believer to his God.[1] Hence, God-talk is really vacuous and nonsense.

It is immaterial whether Basil Mitchell, I.M. Crombie, John Hick and others have succeeded in meeting the challenge of analytic philosophy or not. One thing is clear that believers and non-believers have been talking about God, without seeing the absurdity in their dialogues about God. Hence, 'God-talk is absurd' is itself an absurd statement. But the conclusion of analytic philosophy has followed from the sharpening of the tools of thinking, i.e., by making language as precise as possible. How has the emphasis on the precision of language come about? Nay, more. This precision of language has made God-talk absurd.

Well, this emphasis on the precision of language is not new. It started with Descartes who had laid down the criterion of 'clearness and distinctness', which really characterized the propositions of mathematics. And mathematics was considered to be the most *certain* of sciences. Hence, from Descartes to Kant, scientific knowledge was taken to be the model of knowledge and that is to be found in mathematics and physics. Even much later Sigmund Freud laid down, what is not in science cannot be found anywhere else. Result? God cannot be found by science, for God is a matter of *values* and science deals with facts. Even science and scientific pursuits are based on spiritual quest in man, and, are regarded as sacrosanct. Hence, science cannot be bereft of values, even though it cannot establish values. This is clear from even a cursory glance at the origin of scientific thought in Greece.

Greek thinkers from Thales (624-550 BC) to Plato (429-347 BC), Aristotle (384-322 BC) started the game of free enquiry by discarding religious myths. This was an enquiry from which gods had disappeared. When this free enquiry emerged once again after the fall of Constantinople in 1453, then it started in the investigation of nature (Giordano Bruno b. 1548 and in 1600 he was burnt as a martyr to science, Johann Kepler, 1561-1630); Galileo Galilei (1564-1642). This free scientific enquiry was strengthened by the religious dialogues between the Muslim teachers belonging to the

[1]A. Flew and A. Macintyre eds., *New Essays in Philosophical Theology*, ch. 4 and 6.

university of Cordova in Spain, and the Christian thinkers. In the dispute, they ultimately agreed that not scriptural testimony, but the established facts of nature alone will decide the issues between Islam and Christianity. The Muslim teachers had adopted Aristotle's philosophy. Hence, the Christian thinkers were forced to adopt Aristotelian philosophy, at first through Arabian translation and then later by studying Greek directly through the scattered Greek scholars who had to leave their centre at Constantinople. Thus, at first it was the religious motive which encouraged the study of nature. But the Greek study of nature was inimical to religion, because from the start it had no truck with religion, and arose as a revolt against the prevailing religions.

It was much later on that the atheistic implications of science began to show themselves. Copernicus (1472-1543), Boyle (1626-91) along with Kepler, Galileo and celebrated Isaac Newton (1642-1727) established a mechanical view of the universe. This mechanistic philosophy was further extended to the organic world by Charles Darwin (1809-82) through his theory of Evolution. But quite obviously a machine does not require a soul within it, even though it admits of a mechanist *ab extra*. Hence, Newton as a devout believer in God established deism, according to which theory God having once creating the world has retired from it. This gave rise to the uncomfortable thought that God is no longer concerned with man and his destiny, even though he has created the world in the beginning. Thus science reiterates what La Place had stated long ago on an enquiry by Napoleon, 'Sir, we have no need for God' in science. The two world wars in the twentieth have confirmed this deep scepticism in the Western moderners.

After all, even when deism had banished God from the everyday concern of human life, the thinkers entertained the hope of continued progress as a result of science and technology. However, it was science itself which forged the weapons of war and brought devastation and miseries for the western people, unheard of in the past. Even when peace returned, economic depression sapped the vitality of the moderners and brought in an era of the loss of human values. The second world war with its nuclear devastation simply added to the process of dehumanization of nature and man. The prophets of unlimited progress through science, have turned into prophets of doom in the fourth quarter of the twentieth century. What is true of science is also true of philosophy, in which thinkers become aware of the nascent thought of the people around them. Philosophy is simply the self-consciousness of the age of its ideals and ideologies.

The Western modern philosophy started with Bacon and Descartes. Bacon expressed his delight in *New Atlantis* which is just an utopia on the basis of science and its blessings, but Descartes saw that science gave certain and progressive knowledge in its domain. Why should not a philosopher adopt the methodology of science? Of course, he could not have understood the methodology of science, and even the scientist of his age did not have any philosophical knowledge of science and its methodology. But the scientist knew well how to make use of scientific method and its world-view or presupposition. Not only Descartes, but Spinoza and Leibniz thought mathematics to be a form of science. But mathematics is not science, but is its language. Naturally, Descartes wanted philosophy to adopt *a priori* method of mathematics, for obtaining indubitable truth. But how can through *a priori* knowledge can one obtain any factual knowledge of the world, Soul and God, which are the traditional entities of philosophy?

Even Kant denied the scientific knowledge of God. According to him, science can know the sensible or the phenomena, but not the supersensible or noumena. God is a noumenon. Hence, there can be no science of God. God at most is an object of faith. When we come to the contemporary times, then the logical positivists have simply refined and extended Humean scepticism and Kant's agnosticism in concluding that any God-talk is self-contradictory and absurd. Thus, it is not the fool but the wise, who fully well knowing the notion of God make God-talk impossible.

Hume had laid down much before now that human beings are not guided by reason, but by their natural propensities. Thus, even the wholesale and radical denial of God is really based on human psychology, which can be explained in terms of Jung's theory of Individuation.

We have already referred to Jung's fourfold stages of an individual's evolution, namely, Shadow, Anima-animus, Mana personality and Mandala experience. At each stage there are three fates which one may encounter in becoming a whole. These three processes are of projection, identification and assimilation. For example, at the initial stage of shadow, an individual projects his shadow on some existing entity. The shadow really represents the dark forces within the individual himself, but by projecting on others, he comes to regard a foreigner, a colleague, a neighbour as his enemy, and, begins to take defensive measures against him. But there is another kind of thing which may happen to him in his encounter with his own shadow. He may identify himself with evil forces. He may begin to act in a devilish manner, in utter contrast to his former usual self. This is a process with which Indians are very well familiar. In the process of becoming a yogi, very often the neophyte turns into a pervert or demoniac being. Only by *assimilating* the dark forces personified in the archetype of the Shadow, the individual realises that the dark forces are within his own self. This realisation is accompanied with the release of all the energies hitherto locked up in the Shadow, to be used in further adjustment to the next higher stage of Anima-animus.

Now what is true of the Shadow, is also true of Anima-animus, Mana personality and Mandala experience. At the stage of Anima-animus, the individual has to confront with his sexual urges. After successfully adjusting to them by assimilation, he has to overcome the forces locked up in the worship of Gods, goddesses, saints etc. After fully realising the realities of them, he gets emboldened to deal with the last task of becoming a perfect Self himself, which he was so assiduously seeking in the archetypes of Mana personality. Here the question of projection does not arise, for in this stage all the gods and goddesses have disappeared. But the possibility of identification with the perfect Self remains open. At this occasion of identification with Mandala experience arises the worship of humanity which Augustus Comte sought to popularise. However, the modern man has been deprived of the Glorious Man about whom the sky and earth will sing praise. After the two bitter wars, the modern man has been disillusioned. At most he can advertise and popularise the account of Nietzsche put into the mouth of the mad man declaring that God is dead. The modern man cannot look upon man as an object of worship. He is more to be pitied than glorified. Is he waiting for *the Godot*, or, just waiting for the universal extinction of life?

But waiting for *the Godot* is really, waiting for the God beyond God which Tillich visualized and which the Advaitism of Shankara and Shūnyatā of Nāgārjuna have so eloquently preached with conviction. Again, if a higher picture of the Perfect Self does not emerge, then the modern man waiting for the universal doom will not be 'without religion'. Here too the modern man suffering from a sense of guilt for misusing the gifts of God, is getting aware of the danger of hell-fire in the form of universal extinction.

Thus, living without God is also a matter of religion; only the modern man is disillusioned about his traditional religious moorings. Perhaps he is likely to get new light or *bodhi* in the teachings of Shankara to find that light in which all other lights grow pale. The doctrine of Shūnyatā is not much different from Shankara's state of Mandala experience in which all other dualistic forms of worship are lost and silenced, and, a state of differencelessness is reached. The doctrine of Shūnyatā teaches the same state of realising differencelessness negatively, what the advaitism of Shankara teaches affirmatively. However, affirmation and negation are the two aspects of human being. The affirmative way, runs the risk of idolatry inasmuch as some God (as in Rāmānuja and kindred *bhakti* cults) comes to relapse into the dualistic worship, yielding to what may be called idolatry or anthropomorphism where man, the worshipper, in some form comes to be deified. On the other hand, the negative way of Shūnyatā has the risk of running into vague religiosity and relapsing into all kinds of aberrations with which *Vajrāyana tantra* of Mahāyāna Buddhism came to be characterised. Man cannot live without risk, without anxiety and fears. The task of becoming an authentic man is the rarest of thing and comes from the state of eternal vigilance which is the doctrine of *Gunasthanas*.

Man! Thou are condemned to be religious. Either acknowledge this, or, lead a life of inauthentic existence in which one pretends to be without one's ultimate concern.

The veteran journalist, Khushwant Singh writes in *Telegraph* of October 29, 1983 that all religions are both untrue and harmful:

> "We have been told *ad nauseam* that all religions preach love. We are seldom told that at the same time all religions practise hate. How else can we explain wars in the name of religion? Christians crusading against Muslims, Muslims waging Jihād against non-believers, Hindus engaging themselves in Dharmayuddha against *mlechhas*? Over the last few months our country has provided us ample evidence that no matter how much love religions teach, in actual practice they spread hatred.

How else can we explain riots that have taken place only this year between Hindus and Christians, Muslims and Hindus, Sikhs and Hindus, Shias and Sunnis and pogroms perpetrated on the Harijans? I have never had much respect for religion: I subscribe to Bertrand Russell's view that it has done more harm than good. In his classic expose *Why I am not a Christian*, Russell affirmed his basic conviction: 'I think all the great religions of the world—Buddhism, Hinduism, Christianity, Islam and Communism—are both untrue and harmful.' "

Khushwant Singh is not ignorant of philosophy but he should have known what Freud had written long time ago that love and hate are the two basic drives of man. Religion has been found to be a means of educating the aggressive drive in man. But as yet people do not fully understand the nature of religion and its proper functions, so they begin to proclaim the exclusive claim of religious truth for their brand of faith by denying this privilege to other forms of religion. This causes religious strife and the pugnacity in men, instead of being curbed, gets an opportunity to be fully expressed. Alas! we do not know when man will realise that different labels attached to different religions must go. Shankara preached the religion of differencelessness according to which, all differences are silenced in Brahma-realisation. However, Shankara fully concurred with the *Gītā* (XVII.4) that men use religion tamasically i.e., for their personal gain, worldly prosperity and even for much more lower ends. Here lies the rub. Khushwant Singh and his other like-minded thinkers should also find out means other than religions to curb the pugnacity; greed and beastly passions in men. Much of religion has gone from the lives of the people. But, life has become much worse instead of becoming better. Even Freud, the arch-iconoclast, had to admit the efficacy of religion for maintaining mental health. Religion may be highly inadequate defence against the beast in man, but so far it is the only defence. What we need today is the prevention of the exploitation of religion, specially for political gains.

Religion *a priori* has been assimilated to science. This has produced most erroneous views about religion. Let us be clear about this point.

RELIGIOUS STATEMENTS HAVE NOTHING TO DO WITH TRUTH AND FALSITY

Many theists think that their own respective religion is true, and, all others are either false or only partially true. However, the word 'true' is now applicable only with regard to facts which are given to us by perception or by experimental techniques accepted by the scientists concerned. If the statements with regard to facts are verified, then they are declared as true, or, otherwise they are discarded as false. Now the supreme reality like Brahman or Nirvana is beyond perceptual experience, nay wholly indescribable. Hence, statements concerning Brahman or Nirvana cannot be verified. Therefore, these statements can neither be called true nor false. Even theistic statements are not subject to perceptual experience which can be repeated at will or publicly verified. Therefore, religious statements whether theistic or non-theistic are not factual, and, according to the linguistic usage of the term 'true' cannot be meaningfully applied to them. If religious statements are not subject to verifiable public experience, then how can they be meaningfully used in any religious dialogue?

This problem will be taken up later on, but even now it can be stated that religious statements are faith-statements and they rest their claim on cultivated and disciplined intuition and can be communicated only through the life lived and death died of the believers who make their faith-statements. But once a faith is accepted, its statements are made by having a picture of reality and a consistent use of the terms pertaining to that picture. Such a religious language has been called analogical or symbolical and, its main function is evocative i.e., in arousing a kind of experiences communicated or intuited through symbolical statements. Most probably this will suffice for the time being. But what are the grounds on the basis of which religious statements are not regarded as 'true'?

Well, in the West largely Kant and in the East the Jainas, Buddhists, Mīmāṃsakas and even Rāmānuja have shown all the proofs for the existence of God to be fallacious. It was Kant who first criticized all the proofs for God's existence, one by one. Later on, at the present time. A. Flew, J. Findlay, J.J.C. Smart, B. Russell, A.J. Ayer, H. Reichenbach and so on, have simply refined the sceptical arguments advanced by David Hume.

Most of the modern refutation of theistic proofs is based on the empirical principles of verifiability-falsifiability. There can be no direct verification of God's existence, but John Hick and I.M. Crombie try to take recourse to post-mortem verification. However, post-mortem verification is itself a religious postulate and not an empirical test. Hence, theistic existence cannot be made meaningful in terms of verifiability. Again, theistic statements are not factual, since they are not falsifiable, according to A. Flew on three counts:

1. God is described by words which are killed by thousand qualifications like 'God is love', but this is not parental love or the love of the lover and so on and so forth. Hence, words are emptied of their meaning.
2. Again, a theist is so much committed to God that nothing will really count against theistic assertion.
3. A theist ultimately falls upon metaphysical defence (e.g., F.C. Copleston i.e., human beings have only very fragmentary knowledge of the universe, but the real significance of any event has to be judged in terms of the world as a whole. But metaphysical defence is no defence for the empiricist, since the world as a whole is not an empirical event. Thus *total* explanation of the world cannot be got (B. Russell) or, seeking God beyond the world as its cause is not intelligible. 'Event' is an occurrence within the world and its cause can be asked for. But asking the cause of the world is meaningless, since this kind of cause is not the cause of the world as a whole (which is not an event, but a series of events). One can see in this A.J. Ayer's objection, the echo of Kantian thought according to which the category of cause can be applied legitimately to a phenomenon, but not to a noumenon like God.

Hence, God-talk has been declared to be self-contradictory, absurd and vacuous.[1] The theists have raised many objections against the theory of verifiability-falsifiability which had its basis

[1]A brief reference has been made in my *Introduction to Religious Philosophy*, concerning the views of the thinkers mentioned here in this context. See also *Tractatus*, 6.41; 6 4312.

in Wittgenstein's *Tractatus* 4.024, 5.61, 51.51c M. Schlick had given a very neat statement of verifiability i.e., the meaning of a proposition is the method of its verification. But quite obviously unless one has the prior understanding of meaning of a proposition, one cannot find out the way of verifying it. Hence, 'meaning' has to be distinguished from the 'conditions of verification' of a proposition. Besides, Ludwig Wittgenstein in his later *Philosophical Investigations* stated that there could be different *kinds* of meaning. Religion deals with values and not with facts. Naturally, religious statements have no factual meaning. Hence, elucidating the view of Wittgenstein, W. Donald Hudson maintains that religion has to be taken in its own native habitat and must not be assimilated to science.[1]

> "Whatever believing in God may be, it can't be believing in something we can test; or find means of testing."[2]

The reason is that the meaning of the world cannot be a part of the world. But how to go out of the world to find the meaning of the world? The picture gets a bit complicated. But like Nagasena in *King Milinda's Questions*, Nāgārjuna, Shankara, Wittgenstein have recommended the language of silence. 'What we cannot speak about we must pass over in silence (*Tractatus* 6.54, 7).' One goes beyond verbalization. The second point is that any value-judgment has to be distinguished from factual statements. God is said to be an embodiment of values (H. Hoffding). Hence, any proposition about God is non-factual, so beyond the sphere of truth and falsity.

RELIGIOUS STATEMENTS AS ANALOGICAL, PICTORIAL AND SYMBOLICAL

God and Brahman are Unknown and Unknowable

To know really means to know through the dualistic category of subject and object. Besides, the object of knowledge is initially

[1]W. Donald Hudson, *Wittgenstein and Religious Belief*, pp. 153, 155, 157.
[2]Ibid., p. 156.

visible or sensible. But both in the East and West, theistic or non-theistic deity is not knowable in the ordinary sense of 'knowable', either in terms of common sense or science (i.e., empirically). In the book of Exodus 3:14, Yahwe declares Himself to be 'I am' i.e., He *is*, but not *what* He is. Thomas Aquinas, Kant and Paul Tillich have kept this sense of God in their religious philosophy. For Thomas Aquinas God is transcendent and is only imperfectly knowable analogically or very darkly, almost verging on agnosticism. Again, for Kant, God from the viewpoint of scientific knowledge is unknown and unknowable. At most He is an object of faith. In the same way, Paul Tillich says that all that we can say about God is that He has Being, but apart from this statement anything said about Him is only symbolical.

Even in the New Testament, it has been said that 'No one has seen God' (*Jn*. 1.18), and, St. Paul calls God 'invisible' (*Col*. 1.15). The Book of Job makes a remarkable statement:

> "Can you discover the limits and bounds of the greatness and power of God? The sky is no limit for God, but it lies beyond your reach. God knows the world of the dead, but you do not know it" (Job. 11.7-8).

Then God has been declared to be a 'mystery', not in the sense of a problem which has not been solved till now. But in the sense that He can never enter into the ken of human knowledge. It appears to be a religious category *sui generis*. In Indian philosophy it is called *neti, neti*. Language instead of revealing His nature, really conceals it. For this purpose, yogic sādhanā consists in emptying the mind of all thoughts, so that the pure nature of intelligence, without being parted by the dualistic categories of cognition may be intuitively grasped in the Bergsonian sense i.e., by becoming Brahman itself. We may call it Russell's 'knowledge by acquaintance' *par excellence*. In this sādhanā we shall get the object of supreme religious quest as '*Mysterium fascinans et tremandum*', God remains most mysterious to the person who has the most favoured vision of Him. The topic will come again in the treatment of the subject by L. Wittgenstein who refers to the sphere of 'the mystical'. But it is enough to show that the highest object of religious quest has to be regarded as 'unknown and unknowable', in the sense that God or 'God beyond God' as Brahman or

Nirvana is not a fact, or, in the pregnant statement of Samuel Alexander:

> "God as actually possessing deity does not exist, but is an ideal, is always becoming; God as the whole universe tending towards deity does exist."[1]

R.S. Bhatnagar shows that even the sufis maintain that God is essentially unknowable. Calif Abū Bakr is quoted to have said:

> "Praise to God who hath given His creatures no way of attaining to the knowledge of Him except through their inability to know Him."[2]

The reason is that man is finite and God is infinite; man is a creature and God is his creator. Human intellect is adequate to know the phenomena, but not the noumena. Hence God can be described only negatively, according to Al-Junayd, God is the opposite of what is imaged in the human heart. God is apprehended only through gnosis:

> "Gnosis involves the negation of whatever is reason i.e., whatever notion of God can be formed by reason, God in reality is something different (from it)."[3]

However, the unknowability of the supreme reality called Brahman has been maintained in the Upanishadic thought.

The *Upanishads* form the basic writing of the Hindus, from which all subsequent writers like Shankara, Rāmānuja, Tagore and Aurobindo have drawn their inspiration. The reality for the *Upanishads* is non-dual. It

> "is not this, it is not that (*neti, neti*). It is unseizable, for it cannot be seized" (*BU.*, IV.2.4: See also *BU.*, II.3.6; III.9.26).

[1]S. Alexander, *Mind*, p. 428; *Space, Time and Deity*, vol. II, p. 365; *The Listener*, 3 Dec. 1930, p. 922.

[2]R.S. Bhatnagar, *Dimensions of Classical Sufi Thought*, p. 139.

[3]Ibid., p. 138.

Again:

> ". . . . where knowledge is of a dual nature, there, indeed, one hears, sees, smells, tastes . . . . where knowledge is not of a dual nature, being devoid of action, cause, effect, unspeakable, incomparable, indescribable . . . . what is that? It is impossible to say" (*Maitri*, VI.7; also see *BU.*, II.4.14).

The *Bṛhadāraṇyaka* gives reason for this. Brahman is the supreme condition of knowing, perceiving, remembering etc., and as such cannot be itself perceived, exactly as Kant had stated about 'the *a priori* synthetic unity of apperception':

> "You could not see the seer of seeing. You could not hear the hearer of hearing. You could not think the thinker of thinking. You could not understand the understander of understanding" (*BU.*, III.4.2).

> "Wherefrom words turn back,
> Together with the mind, not having attained."
> (*Taittirīya*, II.4)

And yet Brahman indwells in everything, ... in the sun (*Taittirīya*, II.8; III.10.4), in the fire and the heart (*Maitri*, VI.17; VII.7), yonder and beyond (*BU.*, III.7.1; V.15). Hence, by knowing Brahman one knows *All* (*BU.*, I.4.7). Thus, *Chāndogya* puts it thus (VI.I.4-7):

> "Just as, my dear, by one piece of clay everything made of clay may be known . . . . the modification is merely verbal distinction, a name; the reality is just 'clay'."

What is true of clay and clay-vessels is also true of copper and copper things, iron and iron things etc. Later on, Rāmānuja, true to the spirit of the *Upanishads,* maintains that Brahman is the indwelling and controlling spirit of everything. Hence, again, the *Chāndogya* says:

> "That which is the finest essence—this whole world has that as its soul. That is Reality that is Ātman" (VI.9-16).

Brahman is the key for by knowing it man knows the meaning and purpose of the universe. And yet the meaning of the universe lies beyond the universe as Wittgenstein would say. But man must know this unknowable Brahman, for otherwise he will not find rest until he is attuned to this Brahman by having a glimpse or gnosis of it. This urgency in man is based on the doctrine of religion *a priori* to which reference has already been made. That man is condemned to know the unknowable Brahman is the supreme predicamental situation of man. Groping after the unknowable Brahman, man tries to know it more or less unsuccessfully through analogy, picture, myth-making and symbol.

That which is beyond thought,—beyond verbal descriptions can never be object of religious dialogue. But as a matter of fact even the *Upanishads* do express the invisible and inexpressible. Their language is of *neti, neti* (*Bṛhad.*, II.3.6; III.9.26; IV.2.4; IV.4.22; IV.5.15), or, of silence (*Bṛhad.*, IV.4.52 for a knower becomes *muni*, *Shanta*, *Māṇḍūkya* 7; *Śvetaśvatara* VI.19), or, of paradoxes (*Īsha*, 4.5). Apart from the language of silence, negation and paradoxes the *Upanishads* also resort to the figurative and metaphorical modes of speech. But it would be desirable here to refer to St. Thomas Aquinas and Paul Tillich in the West, and Gauḍapāda and Shankara in India who have devised special techniques in talking about the unutterable and indescribable object of our religious pursuit.

Analogia Entis

According to the angelic doctor, St. Thomas Aquinas (1224-74), God is transcendent to the world, He has created. Now we make various statements about this transcendent God.

Do they apply to Him univocally or negatively or analogically? For instance, God is said to be wise, good and loving. Are these words used in the same sense in which they apply to human beings? St. Thomas does not accept this univocal sense of the terms in relation to God. Nor does he admit that none of these words apply to Him, for this would lead to scepticism. Hence, according to St. Thomas, words derived from the finite segments of human experience apply to God analogically.

The analogical application of words to God is based on the category of cause-effect, or, creator-creature relationship. In other words, to some extent effect throws some light on the nature of cause which gives rise to the effect.[1] In the same way, finite created beings reflect the nature of their creator, namely, God:

> "Terms signify God to the extent that our intellect knows Him. And since our intellect knows God from creatures it knows Him to the extent that creatures represent Him."[2]

The term 'analogy' has been derived from two Greek words *ana* (according to) and *logos* (ratio, proportion) meaning similitude in relationship, in proportion to their respective being or essence. Two kinds of analogical predication have been mentioned, namely, the analogy of *proportionality* and of *Attribution.* According to the analogy of proportionality, the properties of creatures and God are in proportion to their essence e.g.

$$\frac{\text{Intelligence of a dog}}{\text{Dog's being}} : : \frac{\text{Intelligence of a man}}{\text{Man's essence}} : : \frac{\text{Intelligence of God}}{\text{Essence of God}}$$

Of course, both a dog and a man are intelligent, but when a dog is said to be intelligent, it does not mean that he is like a Newton or an Einstein. In relation to his constitutional being, a dog is said to be intelligent even though we know that the highest of dog is much lower than the dullest of man. In the same manner, the intelligence of God far exceeds the intelligence of man; nay so much so that we can describe God only negatively. God's intelligence is not of a Newton or an Einstein or even the greatest human and angelic creature. From the very nature of the case, God's essence is not known. Therefore, to talk of God's intelligence or wisdom is all in vain. All that we can say is that God *is* but not *what* He is.

To mitigate the difficulty arising from the analogy of proportionality, the analogy of attribution has been suggested. This is said to be a weaker form of analogy. Here an attempt is made to

[1]St. Thomas is an Aristotelian, using the concept of cause in the Aristotelian sense as efficient causality with some end in view. Similarly, God is taken to be an architect, who works, according to some design. Hence, the effect reflects the nature of designed causality. Further, God as the prime mover, moving everything without moving Himself, puts God in a different category from the world.

[2]F.C. Copleston, *Aquinas*, p. 129.

predicate something of God positively with the help of terms derived from creaturely relation. For instance, 'love' primarily is used in relation to human beings, but analogically it is attributed to God too. Of course this term 'love' is not spoken of God literally, but only figuratively. It is at most a floor-concept and not a ceiling concept about God. In other words, whatever be the best about human or any creaturely love is only insignificant in relation to divine love. Here again attributes applied to God have to be purified and refined by negation. For this reason, A. Flew opined that any God-talk is killed by a thousand qualifications. Nay, God's love is said to be radically different from anything we know about creaturely relation.

Any God-talk even analogically becomes impossible simply because He is radically different from His creatures. God is not characterized by any internal relation. In Him essence and existence are identical. Naturally no relational mode of speech is possible. Hence, the bitter comment of W.T. Blackstone:

> "But if there are no relations in God, then the relation of attribution is also ruled out. Or, is the relation of attribution itself to be viewed analogically? If so, the theologian is left in uncomfortable position of attributing unknowable properties to an unknowable being, using an unknowable relation of attribution. The 'cloud of unknowing' is a complete overcast."[1]

In the eyes of competent authorities the doctrine of *analogia entis* ends in agnosticism. Reverent silence is the only outcome by treating God as absolutely transcendent. Let us see whether Paul Tillich succeeds in rehabilitating this doctrine, for, according to him his theory of symbolism is only a modern version of *analogia entis*.[2]

Paul Tillich's Theory of Symbolism

Paul Tillich (1886-1966) writes about God exactly as St. Thomas

[1]W.T. Blackstone, *The Problem of Religious Knowledge*, p. 67. At least six journals are devoted to the explication of the theology of St. Thomas Aquinas. 'Analogy' in *The Encyclopaedia of Philosophy*, ed. Paul Edwards; *The Five Ways*, by A. Kenny are important.

[2]Paul Tillich, *Systematic Theology*, vol. I, p. 239.

has described Him:

> "The being of God is being-itself. The being of God cannot be understood as the existence of a being along side others or above others . . . . Even if he is called the 'highest being' in the sense of the 'most perfect' and the 'most powerful' being, this situation is not changed. When applied to God, superlatives become diminutives."[1]

Again, Tillich continues:

> "There is no proportion or gradation between the finite and the infinite. There is an absolute break, an infinite 'jump'."[2]

If there is a complete hiatus between the human and divine, then no God-talk is possible; and, scepticism or agnosticism or even complete indifference to God is the only logical outcome. But Paul Tillich realises that some positive relation has to be established between man and God if any theological account has to be maintained. Here Tillich advances the doctrine of correlation:

> "There is a correlation in the sense of correspondence between religious symbols and that which is symbolized by them. There is a correlation in the logical sense between concepts denoting the human and those denoting the divine. There is a correlation in the factual sense between man's ultimate concern and that about which he is ultimately concerned."[3]

Tillich does not say much about the concept of correlation beyond calling it 'correspondence' which we know to be a vague term. But he really means a 'mutual interdependence' between 'God for us' and 'we for God'. God in his abysmal nature is in no way dependent on man his knowing, but:

> "God in his self-manifestation to man is dependent on the way man receives his manifestation."[4]

[1]Paul Tillich, *Systematic Theology,* vol. I, p. 235.
[2]Ibid., p. 237.
[3]Ibid., p. 60.
[4]Ibid., p. 61.

From a theological viewpoint the divine life is made manifest in revelation. Of course, from the viewpoint of the finite, everything participates in the power of God's Being:

> "This double relation of all beings to being-itself gives being-itself a double characteristic. In calling it creative, we point to the fact that everything participates in the infinite power of being. In calling it abysmal, we point to the fact that everything participates in the power of being in a finite way, that all beings are infinitely transcended by their creative ground."[1]

There is no factual relation between God and man, for God is beyond any existing being, even the highest existent. But man participating in the being-itself knows. It through symbols which result from an encounter of man with God:

> "The word 'God' produces a contradiction in the consciousness, it involves something figurative that is present in the consciousness and something not figurative that we really have in mind and that is represented by this idea. In the word 'God' is contained, at the same time that which actually functions as a representation and also the idea that it is only a representation."[2]

Thus, the figurative way of thinking about God is only a representation, or, what can be called according to Tillich as a symbol. Symbols are double-edged:

> "They are directed towards the infinite which they symbolize and towards the finite through which they symbolize. They force the infinite down to finitude and the finite up to infinity."[3]

For example, when God is symbolized as the 'father', then God is brought down to the human level, but then the human fatherhood is elevated thereby. Thus by treating God as participating in all

[1]Paul Tillich, *Systematic Theology*, vol. I, p. 237.
[2]S. Hook, ed., *Religious Experience and Truth*, p. 315.
[3]Ibid.

beings, and man too thereby participating in God, finds a relationship in which God-talk is possible:

> "The crucial question must now be faced. Can a segment of finite reality become the basis for on assertion about that which is infinite? The answer is that it can, because that which is infinite is being-itself and because everything participates in being-itself. The *analogia entis* is not the property of a questionable natural theology which attempts to gain knowledge of God by drawing conclusion about the infinite from the finite. The *analogia entis* gives us our only justification of speaking at all about God. It is based on the fact that God must be understood as being-itself."[1]

Thus, it appears that Paul Tillich wants to eat his cake yet to have it. If God is being itself, then nothing can really by said of him, for He is beyond essence and existence i.e. beyond verbalization as we find Brahman to be in advaitism or Nirvana in the doctrine of Shūnyatā. Hence, whatever we say about God is only symbolical.[2] Therefore, we are driven to elucidate Tillich's theology of symbolism.

The Theory of Symbolism

The doctrine of symbolism is the most distinctive feature of Tillich's theology. It occupies an important position in his *Systematic Theology*, and has been expressed succinctly in *Dynamics of Faith*. It was also the subject-matter of a symposium in *Religious Exeprience and Truth*, ed. S. Hook, where Paul Tillich opens and closes his paper about his doctrine of symbolism.

'Symbolism' is the language of theology, according to Tillich, but it is also to be found in all cases of an encounter with what man considers to be his ultimate concern. We have already seen that according to Tillich, no hymn being can exist completely without his ultimate concern, which is being itself. This concern expresses itself in one's faith.[3] In this encounter, Being-itself which is the ground of one's being, appears in different figures and

[1]Paul Tillich, *Systematic Theology*, vol. I, pp. 239-40.
[2]Ibid., pp. 238-39.
[3]Paul Tillich, *Dynamics of Faith*, pp. 101, 106, 114, 126-27.

images. And certainly the ground of our being is beyond them. But in having the images of Being-itself, which is unconditioned transcendent underlying everything finite, the recipient, the man of faith also gets transformed. Man is a result of his encounter, uses 'words' about his ground of being, very often called 'God' in religion. 'The word' is both denotative and expressive. As denotative, the word, the symbol *points to* being-itself or God. As expressive, the symbol communicates the personal state of the theist who gives vent to his state of being grasped and gripped with the power of being-itself. A symbol, therefore is a matter of correlation between the theist and his ultimate concern, called God or Being-itself or unconditioned transcendent by Paul Tillich. A symbol is double edged. It opens a dimension of reality which otherwise remains closed to us. At the same time, *pari passu*, it creates a new sensitiveness in the believer, or unlocks a new element of the soul by virtue of which a new perspective is disclosed about reality.[1] In Indian philosophy this is known as *bodhi* or a third eye. A symbol is both true and false about Being-itself. It can be validly affirmed of God inasmuch as it participates in the power of Being. Further, it can be affirmed of God if it adequately represents the power of Being disclosed to the believer in his encounter with the Being. It also has to be negated because God is beyond any finite existence and being. Every finite segment of reality through which a symbol represents Being is transcended in Its Being. On this dual nature of symbol rests the Protestant principle, which must protest against any symbol if it is taken to be Being-itself (i.e., idolatry where a finite segment takes the place of the Infinite transcendent Being). Hence, atheism as a protest against an idolatrous use of a symbol is also explicable. Therefore 'God stands both for the ultimate and also as a representation of the Ultimate'.[2]

In the light of what has been said about a symbol, we can mention the following characteristics of it.

1. A symbol always points to something beyond itself. If a symbol ceases to do so, then a finite segment of reality will come to usurp the place of the divine. This is known as idolatry. To emphasize this point, Tillich mentions another feature of a symbol

[1]Paul Tillich, *Systematic Theology*, vol. I, pp. 122-24; *Dynamics of Faith*, p. 42.
[2]S. Hook, ed., *Religious Experience and Truth*, p. 315.

namely, it must be transparent and self-negating. For instance, a lens helps one to see through it, but lens itself is only a means and it itself is not the object of one's vision. Hence, a symbol helps one to intuit the divine, or, to have an encounter with one's God.

2. A symbol when it points to the divine, then it becomes a true expression, if it participates in the power of God. For example, a flag participates in the power and might of the nation of which it is the representation. Hence, Jesus Christ, Rāma or Krishna are symbols that bring enhancement of power, and, enrichment of the personality of their believers. This feature of a symbol distinguishes it from a sign which points certainly to something beyond itself e.g., red or green signal, but it does not participate in the power of that to which it refers. A sign has denotative but not an expressive meaning.

3. A symbol opens up levels of reality, which are otherwise closed to us, and, *pari passu* unlocks dimensions and elements of our soul which correspond to this hitherto undisclosed dimensions.[1] This is a point which even John Wisdom observed in 1944-45 (*Proceedings of the Aristotelian Society*). According to John Wisdom, no statement about God is experimental predictive and factual. It very often betrays an *attitude* of the believer, largely expressive of his feeling, but his attitude points to the 'recognition of pattern in time easly missed':

> "Things are revealed to us not only by the scientists with microscopes, but also by the poets, the prophets, and the painters."[2]

Tillich would say that even the pattern disclosed is never factual, but is highly symbolical. The pattern in the form of a picture, story, myth (R.B. Braithwaite, L. Wittgenstein) determines the way of agapeistic and moral life.

4. A symbol opens up the hidden depth of our being, because, it appeals to our collective unconscious, which is the source of all human creativity according to C.G. Jung. As the symbol arises from our primordial unconscious, which is shared by mankind in

[1]Paul Tillich, *Dynamics of Faith*, p. 42.

[2]*Classical and Contemporary Readings in Philosophy of Religion and Gods*, p. 417.

common, so it is trans-individual and to that extent is objective. This is what the existentialist would say. 'The most objective is at the same time the most subjective', because it arises from the shared yearning of mankind in the sense of its participation in the collective unconscious. This symbolic representation of Being-itself is objective even in the Kantian sense i.e., a dream which all men dream and must for ever dream is not a dream, but reality. The only difference between Kant and Tillich is that for Tillich this subjective form of symbol forming unconsciousness, characterizing a specific form of religion, is confined to a believing community only. For example, Jesus Christ as a New Being, variously called 'the son of man', 'the son of God', etc. as the saviour of the world is shared by 'the Christian community alone':

> "The religious language, the language of symbol and myth, is created in the community of the believers and cannot be fully understood outside the community."[1]

Again:

> "Symbols which have an especially social function (e.g., political and religious symbols), are created or at least accepted by the collective unconscious of the group in which they appear."[2]

Further, differing from Kant's doctrine or *a priori*, Tillich holds that the symbols are not fixed. Besides, the myth-making collective unconscious keeps on changing in relation to the varying existential concern even within the same believing community. Hence, Tillich mentions another important characteristic of religion.

5. No doubt, according to Tillich a symbol 'cannot function without being accepted by the unconscious dimension of our being', but like any other product of the unconscious, it grows and dies:

> "They (Symbols) grow when the situation is ripe for them, and they die when the situation changes."[3]

[1]Pual Tillich, *Dynamics of Faith*, p. 24; *Religious Experience and Truth*, pp. 302-3.

[2]Paul Tillich, 'Symbols of Faith' in *Philosophy of Religion*, ed. G.L. Abernetty and T.A. Langfor, p. 358; also *Dynamics of Faith*, p. 43.

[3]Paul Tillich, *Dynamics of Faith*, p. 43.

For example, kingship was fairly popular all over the world at the time when the collective unconscious of mankind was very favourable for it. But now it has become obsolete for the people. This point of Tillich is very rich in its various nuances.

The first thing that it explains is the phenomenon of the Death-of-God movement. The traditional symbol of God fails to click the human mentality at the present time. It is neither true nor false. It has become as obsolete as the god *Zeus* or Thor in the West, secondly, it teaches that every symbol is ambiguous. It is 'true' if it is adequate to express the theonomous experience for the believer, but ceases to be so when the symbol ceases to be adequate in the light of the broadened and deepened consciousness of the people, as a result of political changes and economic conditions of the people. This explains both the value and psychological aptness of atheistic attack of the sceptics. The point of Tillich is that every symbol or a religious mythology in which a number of symbols is strung into a story is time-bound and culture-dependent; with the changes in time and prevailing culture, the symbol and myths get outgrown. Hence, R. Bultmann teaches demythologising to get at the ultimacy which every symbol seeks to express. In simple language, every religion must be prepared for self-criticism so that this atheistic principle may so refine the symbol and mythology that the believer may get nearer and nearer his ultimate concern with the adequacy of expression of his symbols.

The above-mentioned point once again shows that Tillich's doctrine of symbols is another version of *analogia entis*, where two negatives are used to refine the analogical words with a view to getting at God who is 'I am' without 'what I am'. Nay, this atheistic principle prevents a believer into falling into idolatry, which consists in taking a finite segment of reality for the infinite Being-itself. Paul Tillich is always in favour of breaking the symbol when it encourages idolatry. Thus, every symbol of God is *relative*.

The relativity of God's symbols follows from the fact that a symbol rises when the mentality is ripe to receive it, and, decays and dies when it fails to elicit any theonomous or momentous experience in believers. Again, the collective unconscious of Krishna believers is not the same as that of Christian believers. This relativity of a symbol follows from its very nature as an amalgam of the finite-infinite. Every symbol being finite has to be negated by the Infinite Being-itself to which it points, and, yet being a participant in Being-itself has to be asserted of Being-itself:

> "The segment of finite reality which becomes the vehicle of a concrete assertion about God is affirmed and negated at the same time. It becomes a symbol, for a symbolic expression is one whose proper meaning is negated by that to which it points. And yet it also is affirmed by it, and this affirmation gives the symbolic expression an adequate basis for pointing beyond itself."[1]

Hence, the ambiguous character of a symbol accounts for its breaking up called by Tillich atheistic principle, and, also the relativity of all symbols. Knowing this a believer has to be prepared for tolerance, when an atheist breaks up his symbol of God, and, also has to be tolerant in regard to other symbol of God, accepted by the various other believing communities. This will serve as the ground for a league of religious faith in mutual dialogue:

> "Faith must unite the tolerance based on its relativity with the certainty based on the ultimacy of its concern."[2]

In this strain, Tillich succinctly writes about the *relative* character of Christianity:

> "The Christ is God-for-us. But God is not only for us, he is for everything created."[3]

Then again:

> "Christianity as Christianity is neither final nor universal. But that to which it witnesses is final and universal."[4]

Finally for our purpose, Tillich writes about: the New Being in Jesus Christ which is the centre of history for Tillich, the momen-

[1]Paul Tillich, *Systematic Theology*, vol. I, p. 239.
[2]Paul Tillich, *Dynamics of Faith*, p. 57.
[3]Paul Tillich, *Systematic Theology*, vol. II, p. 100.
[4]Ibid., vol. I, p. 134.

tous event for mankind:

> "The words of Jesus and the apostles point to this New Being; they make it visible through stories, legends, symbols, paradoxical descriptions, and theological interpretations. But none of these expressions of the experience of the final revelation is final and absolute itself. They are all conditioned, relative, open to change and additions."[1]

In the concluding section of *The Courage To Be*, Tillich teaches that 'God above God' is the only ultimate source of religion. This source cannot be described in the way the God of all forms of theism is described:

> ". . . . if God encounters man God is neither object nor subject and it is therefore above the scheme into which theism has forced him."[2]

The real religious belief is rooted in the God who appears when God has disappeared in the anxiety of doubt. Hence, 'God above God' is beyond all description and verbalisation:

> "It is not a place where one can live, it is without the safety of words and concepts, it is without a name, a church, a cult, a theology. But it is moving in the depth of all of them."[3]

Here the reader is reminded of Shankara's Brahman to which all symbols of God in the form of Viṣṇu, Rāma, Krishna and Shiva point. But they all have to be negated being born of nescience, in favour of undifferenced Brahman. Then all scriptures and even *mahāvākyas* have to be denied when once the seeker gets a full intuition of Brahman. Before taking up the theological view of Shankara, we should do well to take up other features of Tillich's thought which have some more startling resemblance with Shankara's philosophy.

[1]Paul Tillich, *Systematic Theology*, vol. I, p. 151.
[2]Paul Tillich, *The Courage To Be*, p. 180.
[3]Ibid., p. 182.

The 'Truth' of Symbolic Statements

The word 'truth' is used now to refer to factual truth, or, the truth with regard to a sensible events. God is an infinite reality and cannot be given in empirical experience. Hence, no factual truth is possible with regard to a symbolical statement:

> "The truth of a religious symbol has nothing to do with the truth of the empirical assertions involved in it, be they physical, psychological, or historical."[1]

The reason is that the ultimate concern which is the referent underlying all forms of religious talks, is beyond subject-object differentiation. However, a finite being has to talk about his infinite concern, and, when he talks about it, he can do this only in terms of symbols and myths.[2] But we have already seen that a symbol is a subject-object amalgam. Like Kant, Tillich would say, that a religious community sees reality coloured and shaped by its conscious-unconscious mentality as the receptacle of the divine. Tillich is fully aware of his stand on the ambiguity of his symbol, God-man relationship, and, even the very process of knowing on which symbols depend, is infected with ambiguity.

The whole knowing process has been styled as the ultimate concern of man. But what is the nature of this concern? Is it subjective or objective? The term 'ultimate concern' unites a subjective and an objective meaning for Tillich.[3] The reason is obvious a symbol opens up a new dimension of reality and *pari passu* a new sensitivity and receptivity is created in the user of the symbol. This ambiguity relates to God Himself who is the object of man's ultimate concern:

> "The statement that God is Being-itself is a non-symbolic statement. It does not point beyond itself."
>
> "However, after this has been said, nothing else can be said about God as God which is not symbolic."[4]

[1]Paul Tillich, *Systematic Theology,* vol. I, p. 240.
[2]Ibid., p. 223.
[3]Ibid., vol. III, p. 130.
[4]Ibid., vol. I, pp. 238-39.

As any talk about God is symbolic, hence not literal; so anything about man also is ambiguous. The very essential being of man is the unity of his finitude with the infinitude.[1] Hence, a symbol seeks to bridge the gulf between the finitude of man felt as anxiety and the ground of his being. Therefore, a symbol may be called true when it is the expression of a true revelation:

> "In the history of religion revelatory events always have been described as shaking, transforming, demanding, significant in an ultimate way."[2]

Thus under the influence of one's ultimate concern. Being-itself is variously pictured and symbolized, and, in the advaitic way, Being-itself is called a white canvas on which symbols are projected by way of grasping what eludes and yet lures us. All gods and symbols are mere projections on this white canvas:

> ". . . . projection always is projection on something—a wall, a screen, another being, another realm. Obviously, it is absurd to class that on which the projection is realized with the projection itself. A screen is not projection; it receives the projection. The realm against which the divine images are projected is not itself a projection. It is the experienced ultimacy of being and meaning."[3]

Symbolizing is an ever self-transcending experience in which the eternal is imaged in what is particular and transitory, and, the transitory is viewed in the light of the eternal:

> "In this kind of knowledge the ambiguities of subjectivity as well as objectivity are overcome; it is a self-transcending cognition which comes out of the centre of the totality and leads back to it."[4]

Hence, this kind of knowledge, facing disruption by the ambiguities of symbols, cannot be called true or false. However, other cate-

[1]Paul Tillich, *Systematic Theology*, vol. I, p. 61.
[2]Ibid., p. 110.
[3]Ibid., p. 212.
[4]Ibid., vol. III, p. 225.

gories may apply to it. Symbolic statements:

> "are authentic or unauthentic with respect to their rise; they are adequate or inadequate with respect to their expressive power; they are divine or demonic with respect to their relation to the ultimate power of being."[1]

As said before the divine encounter resulting in revelation is always a shaking experience, momentous and living. If the symbolic statement does not prove to evoke such an experience in speaker-hearer, then it is not authentic. In the language of Tillich, if the symbolic statement describes and evokes a surface instead of one's depth, or, if it is an expression of subjectivity without registering a fact of encounter with reality, then it is unauthentic.[2] In other words, if a symbol instead of participating and pointing to the ultimate Transcendent in a transparent manner, takes the place of the infinite, then it becomes idolatry. An authentic symbolizing brings *'peace and pistis'* as C.G. Jung has pointed.[3] It is always an elevating experience[4] and transforms the individual.[5] A true symbol integrates the personality, but its reverse is a demonic expression leading to the disintegration of the personality,[6] as has also been pointed out by C.G. Jung.

The authenticity of a symbolical statement is quite different from empirical verification. The authenticity in contrast has to be evaluated in terms of the life process itself, without disruption.[7] Nay the authenticity is to be evaluated in terms of the history, tradition and the test of modernity in relation to a believing community. There is always the risk of missing the being-itself as involved in symbol, or, taking the deity to be mere symbol, or, mistaking the Ultimate Concern as one's surface being.

Thus, Paul Tillich's theology supports the view that religious statements are not true or false, but they may be called genuine-

[1]'Symbols of Faith' in *Philosophy of Religion*, eds., G.L. Abernethy and T.A. Langfor, p. 409.

[2]Paul Tillich, *Systematic Theology*, vol. III, p. 64.

[3]Ibid., vol. II, pp. 166-67.

[4]Ibid., vol. I, p. 113.

[5]Ibid., p. 96.

[6]Ibid., p. 102.

[7]S. Hook, ed., *Religious Experience and Truth*, p. 137.

fake, authentic-unauthentic, adequate-inadequate. Once again whilst passing, we note that for Tillich, man, religious language and knowledge are all infected with ambiguities, nay, with paradoxes and self-transcendence. Naturally no literal truth can be attained with regard to the ground of our being, 'God beyond God'. What F.H. Bradley, Nāgārjuna, Gauḍapāda and Shankara would say that no thought with dualistic mode of expression is adequate with regard to reality, is found in Tillich. Again, the statement called 'suicide of thought' by Bradley, 'Silence of Nāgāsena', and the crescendo of *neti, neti* of the *Upanishads* are also echoed by Tillich. In our previous quotation from *The Courage To Be* (p. 182) we find that Being-itself is beyond words and concepts. When one once gets its intuition in its unconditionedness, one goes without cult, without Church and theology. Does it not sound like the advaitic doctrine that by being helped by the illusory scriptures and *mahāvākyas*, one ultimately is awakened into the experience of differenceless Brahman? Tillich criticized Advaitism and Buddhism, without confronting them, because he felt into their lure. Strange it may sound, but Ludwig Wittgenstein too recommends a religious culture of the mystical and silence as the ground for reconciling tension, conflict and competition between the warring camps of religion. Hence, now we take up 'Wittgenstein on religion.'

The Religious Philosophy of Ludwig Wittgenstein

There is little doubt that Wittgenstein's philosophy dominates the whole of Anglo Saxon thought in the last fifty years. Much of Bertrand Russell, A.J. Ayer, G. Ryle, John Wisdom, J.N. Findlay, A.G.N. Flew and so on, can be shown in their distinctive features, as coming under the influence of Wittgenstein. The contributions of Wittgenstein fall into the three periods of *Tractatus Logico-Philosophicus, Blue and Brown Books* and *Philosophical Investigations.* Wittgenstein has not written really specially about religion or theism, but his views can be gleaned from his doctrine about 'the mystical' in *Tractatus*, and in his lecture notes which have been gleaned by his pupils. Here the account of Wittgenstein's thought on theism or God leans heavily on *Wittgenstein and Religious Belief* by W. Donald Hudson.

The *Tractatus* has been interpreted as teaching the doctrine of atomic propositions and atomic simples. To know the meaning of a proposition, one has to analyse it into elementary propositions, which are logically descriptive of atomic simples of reality. The arrangement between the simples is faithfully pictured by the proposition. Could there be any example of the simple? Wittgenstein could not point to any simple, but for him, the simple can be shown for all practical purposes by pointing to 'this blue' or 'this red'. In this teaching of simples and elementary propositions one finds the basis of *logical positivism*, 'the sense-data theory', and the doctrine of precision of language in describing the thing through propositions. Indeed, Wittgenstein had clearly laid down the principles of verifiability-falsifiability (*Tractatus*, 4.024, 5.5151c and 5.615, which were later on widely used by A. Flew and others in showing religious statements to be nonsense.

But slowly and gradually Wittgenstein ceased to emphasize the doctrine of atomic simples and elementary propositions corresponding to them, since he saw that elementary propositions form a system e.g., take the proposition.

This is two feet long.

Quite obviously this is intelligible in reference to the measurement of lengths, and not apart from it. Again, 'this is red' is intelligible only in relation to the whole spectrum of colour.

In *Investigations*, Wittgenstein treated propositions as forming a system, and, not in isolation, in order to determine their meaning: This doctrine of proposition systems has given rise to the doctrine of language-game, which was explicitly stated by Wittgenstein in his *Investigations*. Some Wittgenstein scholars think that Wittgenstein by his doctrine of language-game has refuted his earlier theses of atomic propositions and simples, advaned in the *Tractatus*. Others think that the doctrine of language-game and that the meaning of a proposition lies in its use are really implicit in Wittgenstein's teaching about the rules of grammar and syntax rules in the *Tractatus* itself (3.311, 3.325, 3.326 and 3.327). For us here, it is immaterial to decide whether *Investigations* is really a continuation or refutation of the *Tractatus*. It is enough for us to note that the doctrine of language-game and the meaning of a proposition in its use, sounded the death-knell of a logical positivism of A.J. Ayer's brand, and the refutation of theistic statements in terms of verifiability-falsifiability which is appropriate for determining the meaning of empirical statements in science alone. This also paved the way of thinking that religious statements cannot be assimilated to scientific propositions. Naturally the refutation of theistic statements in terms of logical positivism and the test of verifiability-falsifiability have become irrelevant in the light of later Wittgenstein. Let us start with the doctrine of simples and putative meaning of propositions.

What is a simple? Even in the *Tractatus*, Wittgenstein was not sure of its empirical basis, but he felt then that it could be logically possible in principle. But in the *Investigations*, he clearly saw that the question of finding a simple is asked only in regard to a complex situation e.g., we may be asked to find the simples in a chess-board. But what is meant by a simple here? Do we mean the white and black squares of which the chess-board is composed? Or, do we mean the simples in relation to colour patches or the physical parts of the chess-board? Hence, a simple can be determined only with reference to a specific context. This is still more clear in his further doctrine of the meaning of proposition in terms of use and usage.

Side by side of the doctrine of atomic simples, Wittgenstein attacked the teaching of precision of language. When one is asked to come at 8 a.m., then how is the exact time to be determined? By whose watch? Does it matter if one turns up one minute later or earlier? Hence, language works equally well with some indefiniteness. The importance of this observation has to be evaluated with reference to *Clarity is not Enough*, by H.H. Price, or, F. Waismann's *How I See Philosophy*.

Even in the *Tractatus*, Wittgenstein had remarked that the meaning of an expression depends on the rules of grammar or syntax. Quite obviously, it means that ultimately rules of syntax depend on the way in which we use our language. But once the emphasis from referents is withdrawn and 'use' is emphasized, then the importance of context comes to the forefront. A word means this or that, depends on training and context. For example, when a carpenter asks his helper to bring a screw, then he supposes that the helper has learned the meaning of 'screw' as something different from a nail, and, that he also knows the size and kind of screw in the context of the situation. Nay, more.

Language as a whole is a complex of different kinds of language games which are distinct and yet interdependent. For example, the language-game of science is quite different from the rules of religious language, though they are interrelated. Each language-game has its own end and is governed by its own tools (i.e., technical terms) guided by its rules of usage. Every end has its relation to one's form of life and its activities. The forms of life in which we participate constitute, in some important way the intelligibility and justifiability of what we say. One need not therefore seek for still some other criterion of meaning.[1] A religious language, therefore, is intelligible in its own sphere, within its own community of believers, as Paul Tillich too has emphasized. It would be a category-mistake if we mix different tools of language guided by their respective rules of syntax. In other words, the language-game of religion must not be confused with that of science. The criterion of truth and meaning of religious statements is quite different from that of empirical propositions. What the theologians, specially R. Otto said about the *sui generis* character of religion, has been maintained by Wittgenstein by his analysis of language.

The message of the *Tractatus* ends in his doctrine of the mystical, which if W. Donald Hudson is to be trusted, formed the real meaning and importance of the book. Hence, we now turn to 'the mystical'.

From the above account, it is clear that Wittgenstein sought to know reality through the analysis of language. In the *Tractatus*, Wittgenstein brought into focus the language of science which deals with facts or sensible events. But values and the meaning of life are not facts. Do they come under reality? Wittgenstein would admit that in our linguistic behaviour we do talk about God, morality and the meaning of life. If language is at all a guide to reality, then these values have also to be regarded as objective. But what is the difference between the objective facts and the objectivity of values? The objectivity of values of God shows itself, but cannot be said. What is the sense of saying 'shows itself'? The value, called beauty is something with which an artist is concerned. He paints a landscape or setting sun, which one sees and can describe. But the way he paints can never be painted or described. It nevertheless shows itself in his paintings. The same can be said about logical form, according to Wittgenstein, even in his *Tractatus*:

"Propositions cannot represent logical form! it is mirrored in

[1] W. Donald Hudson, *Wittgenstein and Religious Belief*, p. 55.

> them . . . . what expresses *itself* in language, we cannot express by means of language. Propositions *show* the logical form of reality . . . ."
>
> "What can be *shown*, cannot be said." (4.12—41212).

Thus, there are two kinds of statements, one kind is factual, and the other valuative. Quite obviously, beauty cannot be a matter of fact, but it shows itself in the sculpture of beauty or a painting of a landscape. Hence, in talking about God, one cannot point his finger and say 'Look! here is God'. But the stories about Jesus, his parables and death are the means to evoke in the believer to experience the mystical,—one's God. In the same way, the story of Lord Krishna, nay even his pranks are the means to experience one's God, as we find in devout Ālvārs of South India (about 600-800 AD). If a Christian cannot experience God through the story, parables and death of Jesus, then he cannot experience God. If one does not see Krishna *in* the stories, exploits and *līlā,* one cannot be a devotee of Krishna. But what about the stories themselves? Are they empirical or historical. To the extent they are historical, they are not religious. The *Bible,* the *Mahābhārata* as exhibiting the spiritual, the divine presence, are not historical. In other words, their historicity is irrelevant for religious purposes. As non-factual spiritual events, they are factually nonsense. But then why should we use the nonsensical statements for taking us to the divine? Here Wittgenstein expresses himself in language, which is distinctive of the advaitic language about *mahāvākyas* or the scripture:

> "My propositions serve as elucidations in the following: anyone who understands me eventually recognizes them as nonsensical, when he has used them—as steps—to climb up beyond them. (He must, so to speak, throw away the ladder after he has climbed it up)" (*Tract.* 6.54).

Thus, that which shows itself in religious stories, myths, parables and *līlā* is not a matter of fact. It is a matter which we experience in the depth of our soul, ... it is that which affects our thoughts, actions and profoundly transforms the lives of those who mean them in their spiritual strivings. Let us further try to elucidate what shows itself or the mystical.

The problem of the mystical is of the same nature as 'the sense of the world', or 'ethical values', or 'the problems of life and death, God, and so on'. Quite clearly the meaning of life and death cannot refer to any one event or even a series of events factually. It shows itself in religious stories, great dramas, poetry and so on. But this showing through a segment of the empirical world is at most illustrative, but not descriptive. In the words of Paul Tillich, no symbols can take the place of what is symbolized, though they participate in the symbolandum and *point* to it. But if one wants to point his finger to the 'It', which is the common referent underlying all religious symbols, then one finds *nothing*. In the words of Shankara, the world, the scripture and *mahāvākyas* are illusory, but they lead to the colourless white canvas on which all these phenomenal pictures are thrown or projected. In other words, God is not a sensible fact. According to Wittgenstein, when one has thrown away the ladder through which one has been led to experience God, one has to remain silent. Because there is nothing to describe. This language of silence follows from another consideration.

For Wittgenstein, to know a thing one has to know what it is not. This was noted by Hegel too, for according to Hegel and later Hegelians' every affirmation implies its negation. But at the hands of Wittgenstein, through Einstein and Karl R. Popper,[1] the test of negativity or falsifiability became an important criterion of the empiricity of a statement. According to Wittgenstein:

> "In order for a proposition to be capable of being true, it must also be capable of being false" (*Tractatus*).

Again:

> "The positive proposition necessarily presupposes the existence of the negative propositions and *vtce versa*" (*Tractatus* 5,5151c).

Hence, to know the world as a whole is also to know what the world as a whole is not. But clearly nobody knows what it is to mean that the world does not exist. Naturally, it is nonsense to say, that the world has been produced by a First Cause. Is the

[1]Karl R. Popper; *The Logic of Scientific Discovery*, p. 314.

first cause within or without the Universe? If within, then it cannot be prior to the world; if out of the world, then there can be nothing beyond the world of which we can speak. This is the sphere of silence:

> "what we cannot speak about, we must pass over in silence" (*Tractatus* 6.54, 7).

By consigning God-talk to silence, did Wittgenstein mean that God-talk is nonsense. as A.J. Ayer, A. Flew and others maintained, or, did he mean that God-talk is simply trivialized, once we begin to talk about Him? According to W. Donald Hudson, by remaining, silent about God did not mean for Wittgenstein that God-talk is nonsense. He simply meant that any talk about God would trivialize Him. Once we talk about God, we bring him *on par* with spatio-temporal events, and no part of the world can be the sense of the world:

> "It is logically impossible for the sense of the world to be itself a part of the world, since the meaning of anything cannot be a part of that of which it is the meaning" (*Tractatus* 6, 41).

Again:

> "The solution of the riddle of life in space and time lies outside space and time" (6.4312).

Finally:

> God does not manifest Himself in the World (*Tractatus* 6.432).

Here the views of the four epoch-making thinkers, namely. Nāgārjuna, Shankara, Paul Tillich and Wittgenstein totally agree. Lord Buddha would say, that any talk about God is *avyakta* i.e., metaphysical heresy. Nāgārjuna would say that talk about God would lead to the inherent self-contradiction involved in the categories of thought. Shankara would say that any talk about God, ends in dualism, and, no dualistic talk can lead to non-dual Brahman, Thus, Nagasena replied to king Milinda, 'Sir, Nirvana is silence' (*Nirvanam Shantam*): Thus, according to Wittgenstein, the moment we talk about the mystical, corruption sets in. Hence the mystical must be protected by silence.[1] Hence, religious faith, for Wittgenstein, is unutterable and wordless. In this wordless faith, all the conflicting faiths are reconciled.[2] We would say that Shankara's doctrine of differenceless Brahman succeeds in reconciling all the discords involved in every form of dualistic worship. But Wittgenstein adds something more.

From the above account it is clear that Wittgenstein maintains that religious assertion must not be assimilated to empirical statements either of everyday life or science. The intelligibility and justifiability of religious discourse are restricted to its language-game. On what does this language-game depend? It depends on the picture which the believing community has of its God. Here one should be once again reminded that this picture does not picture that to which it points. That to which this picture refers is Shūnyatā, a nothing, for God is not an existent thing of the world. For example, when various Venuses are carved out of stone, as representing an incomparable beauty, then certainly there is no actual woman which is either carved out of marble or painted. Similarly, when we draw a picture of God in the person of Jesus or Krishna or Lord Buddha, then they do point to something as ultimate reality. Paul Tillich would say that Jesus points to 'God beyond God' ultimately, and, Shankara would say that Lord Krishna points to Brahman, or a Nāgārjuna would say that Lord Buddha refers to Nirvana which is void and nothing, a pure silence. But the divine picture matters, for it affects the believer, the user of the picture from the very depth of his being. From the picture issues forth commitment to actions and deep affectivity. Religious beliefs following from the picture in use are firm and so firm that they may be held even against evidence to the contrary:

> "And religious belief does imply a willingness to change one's whole life. It is not, or not simply, a matter of assenting to certain propositions for which there is deemed to be good evidence, but of being readly to risk everything for the sake of one's beliefs."[3]

[1]W. Donald Hudson, *Wittgenstein and Religious Belief*, p. 106.
[2]Ibid., p. 104.
[3]Ibid., pp. 170-71.

Hence, religious beliefs tacked on the picture are not only as stable as the 'blik' of R.M. Hare, but are held with a great deal of concern. In the words of William James, they are lively, forced and momentous. It is this point of concern which is lacking in John Wisdom's parable of an invisible gardener about whom the believing and non-believing travellers discuss.

Here one is likely to be reminded of R.B. Braithwaite's empirical theory of religious assertions, according to which religious assertions entail a certain behaviour policy, coming under a general moral principle, backed by a story. Here Braithwaite is in agreement with Wittgenstein inasmuch as the story in a religious belief becomes a psychological energiser of moral commitment and self-involvement, but the story also stands for rational justification for all religious acts, expression of gratitude, steadfastness in faith and depth of feeling. According to W. Donald Hudson, Wittgenstein meant that believers should learn the technique of using their religious picture in the following way:

1. Psychological techniques of concentration so that the picture may remain steadied in one's concentration.

   This technique of concentration has been perfected in Jainism, Buddhism and Yoga. The technique refers to the use of a support (*ālambana*) in relation to which concentration is steadied and further refined.
2. Persuasion—Keeping the picture in the centre, the believer preaches his religious faith with a view to invoking/evoking religious feeling within himself and others. This aspect of the use of the religious picture corresponds to *manana* (deep reflection) in Indian philosophy.
3. Drawing certain loosely related logical connections. For example, God in Christian picture is styled as 'rock of ages', shield and shelter against all sufferings', 'eternal mountain', 'living waters', and so on.
4. In drawing certain connections, one has to develop an eye to recognise what is, and what is not appropriate. For instance, God is pictured as a Person, but He is not represented as an embodied being. This was a point hotly defated by the atheists in Indian philosophy:

"To use the picture is, on the one hand, to adduce the kind

> of evidence of its appropriateness; and, on the other, to make inferences from it which are appropriate to the occasion."[1]

Thus, religious talk is rational, though reasoning here is not as rigorous as in science.

If one keeps to religion *a priori*, then there can be really no unbelievers, but there can be various kinds of believers, having different picture:

1. Religious believers differ from one another in using their respective pictures as explanatory of what happens to them and affects them deeply in their lives.
2. Each picture is commissive, for it transforms the whole tenor of the life of the believer and helps him to form his value-judgments and decisions he makes for a certain course of action.
3. The use of the picture determines the feeling tone of the personality of the believer. In other words, it determines mental peace, quiescence or at times even morbid broodings.

What we call as 'unbeliever' is really that person who has outgrown the use of the picture in vogue in his believing community i.e., the picture for him has become obsolete. In other words, as Paul Tillich says, the symbol dies its natural death. Or, it may happen specially in the days of decadence, as in modern India today, that the picture is so repulsive that believers in their own interest do not try to mention it. For instance, many politicians really picture God as a rich minister wielding immense power. This is really a demonic use of the religious picture. This observation about the nature and use of religious pictures calls forth for some critical remarks about the theories of religion by Paul Tillich Wittgenstein and Shankara.

Paul Tillich, Wittegenstein and Shankara

We have given a brief outline of the religious philosophy of Paul Tillich and Ludwig Wittgenstein, because it will show the modern relevance of Shankara, who in our thinking holds the key to a world of philosophy of religion. In our way of evaluation, the picture theory of Wittgenstein is very important, which can be easily assimilated to Paul Tillich's symbology. Wittgenstein's theory of language-game has prevented his followers in regarding God-talk

[1]W. Donald Hudson, *Wittgenstein and Religious Belief*, p. 190.

to be nonsense. Further, his theory of religious silence is important as it can be easily assimilated to Shankara's doctrine of differenceless Brahman where all theistic talks meet and end. But in the end we can conclude with David Pears thus:

> "Wittgenstein's defences of religion and morality are cryptic, inhibited, possibly unhappy and certainly for the most part not original."[1]

Though not original, yet Wittgenstein's theory of religion where picture is said to picture *nothing*, and, that, in religious *silence* one has the best prospect of ending all kinds of theistic dispute, will be highly deemed by Shankara's scholars.

Paul Tillich has been accused as a Shankarite, because of close similarity of views of Tillich and Advaitism. Tillich like the advaitins maintains that no segment of the existent can be attributed to the supreme reality, for Being-itself is beyond essence (though) and existence. This is akin to Shankara's doctrine of Nirguṇa or differenceless Brahman. Why nothing of symbols and existent facts can be attributed to Being-itself? Because all thoughts and finite things, including human minds are ambiguous and infected with internal tension.[2] This is tantamount to saying that thoughts and finite things are illusory and tainted, even though they are sustained by the power of Being.

Again, like Shankara, Tillich also maintains that there is a protestain principle which keeps on protesting against a symbol which no longer continues to be psychologically and ontologically effective for the believers. But Tillich does not give reasons for the atheistic principle. It appears that the collective unconscious and conscious of the believing community, alone explain the birth and death of a symbol: Against this the *Gītā*, Gauḍapada and Shankara mention that it is the pull of Brahman which impels the seeker to rise, step by step, to have the final intuition of Being-itself. Naturally this atheistic principle of Advaitism posits a hierarchy of symbols, where *tāmasic* symbols through the *rājasic* have to give

[1]David Pears, *Wittgenstein*, p. 183. This was written when the works of Wittgenstein's pupils with regard to religion were not taken into consideration. Again, though not original some contributions of Wittgenstein proved very valuable for a philosophy of religion.

[2]Paul Tillich, *Systematic Theology*, vol. I, p. 14; vol. III, p. 130.

way to *sāttvic* symbols, and even the *sāttvic* symbols have to be denied in the final ascent in one's religious pursuit. According to Advaitism, like Paul Tillich and Wittgenstein, it is maintained that Brahman is wordless and can be described as 'Silence'. Only by positing 'silence' in realising Brahman, one has the best prospect of absorbing all theistic forms of religious discourse. In our opinion, Tillich clearly points out this in *The Courage To Be*, (p. 182) be cause on the realisation of 'God above God', one reaches a place at last which is without the safety of words, church or cult or theology. Corresponding to this statement is the Mandala experience of C.G. Jung. Thus the doctrine of Brahma-realisation is powerfully suported by C.G. Jung, Wittgenstein and Paul Tillich.

Tillich does not mention the hierarchy of symbols, even though he classifies them, but without a hierarchy it is difficult to explain the higher and lower symbols in religion, and the atheistic principle inherent in any symbol whatsoever. There is another inexplicable element in Tillich's religious philosophy. He asserts that the power of Being sustains and supports all finite things, and yet Being-itself is beyond them. Tillich maintains that Being-itself participates in all finite things and yet he also maintains that there is an absolute break between them (*Systematic Theology*, vol. I, p. 237). In our opinion, Shankara's theory of *A-jñāna* explains this hiatus between the finite and Being-itself better. The phenomena are all illusory, according to Shankara, but they are thrown against the blank and colourless canvas of Brahman. But, of course Shankara too is constrained to maintain that the finite soul participates in Brahman (enclosure metaphor like *ghatakasha* and *mathakasha*, and even in reflection theory, reflection participates in the self-luminous Brahman). Shankara would say that the whole world of finite things is *anirvacanīya* (indescribable), and Tillich would say that one has to admit the final ambiguity of finite-infinite entities. Has not Shankara said this in terms of 'inexplicability' much better? But it is time now for us to take up the religious philosophy of Shankara.

2

The Religious Philosophy of Shankara

INTRODUCTION

Shankara's religious philosophy is wholly monistic, for the teaches the absolute reality of Brahman which is non-dual, eternal, unproduced and unproducing, changeless and without any modification without any outside or inside. It is beyond any speech and thought and is wholly indescribable. In any literal sense Brahman is without any cause and effect, and remains unaffected by anything.

Whatever information men have about Brahman has been conveyed to them through the scriptures, the most important of which is the *prasthana-traya,* comprising the *Upanishads*, the *Gītā* and Badarāyana's *Brahmasūtra.*[1] As these sources are full of contradictory statements, so different interpretations of their passages have given rise to the various schools of the Vedānta. Again, Shankara's use of the scriptural authorities mentioned above at once distinguishes Vedānta from Jainism and Buddhism which do not regard *prasthana-traya* as authority.

Again, Shankara advances the three paradigm cases of indefinite perception (*nirvikalpaka pratyakṣa*), *suṣupti* and *turīya* for illustrating the reality of objectless pure consciousness (*cit*) that Brahman is. Schools of the Vedānta are divided amongst themselves with regard to the analysis of the paradigm cases mentioned above. But no true understanding of Shankara's Advaitism is possible without the psycho-physiological account of these three states.

As Brahman is without any cause and effect, so Advaitism does not subscribe to *asatkāryavāda* held by the Nyāya-Vaiśeṣika and by some Buddhist schools. As Brahman is wholly-changeless, so

[1]Unless otherwise mentioned the English translation of *The Thirteen Principle Upanishads* by R.E. Hume, has been used. Again, unless otherwise mentioned, the English translation of *Brahmasūtrabhāṣya of Shankara* by George Thibaut *SBE,* vols. 34, 38 has been used. It has been abbreviated as *Vedānta Sūtra.*

even *satkāryavāda* is not fully acceptable. However, *satkāryavāda* has two kinds, namely, *pariṇāmavāda* and *vivartavāda*. Shankara would accept *vivartavāda* which means apparent or seeming changes of the cause. But the word 'apparent' shows that there are no real changes in and of Brahman. With regard to this nature of causation there is much controversy in the Vedāntic schools.

But the most important point of controversy is about the reality of gods or God. Shankara does not favour polytheism and is not unequivocal with regard to theism. However, he favours *mahāvākyas* for obtaining intuition of Brahman. By knowing Brahman one becomes Brahman, and, by becoming Brahman one overcomes all differences of everyday life. Most probably this is the most important teaching in any religious philosophy whatsoever, according to this book.

Further, the schools of the Vedānta are divided over the problems of māyā, the locus of māyā, about the means and destiny of release and some such kindred subjects.

With the problems stated above, we can now briefly outline the system of Shankara.

Shankara's Monistic Philosophy of Brahman

Shankara teaches the monistic reality of Brahman alone, denying at the same time the ultimate reality of Īshvara, jivas and the world.

Shankara resorts to the *Upanishads* in support of his monism. No doubt the *Upanishads* teach also the doctrine of a personal Brahman. However, Shankara selects those passages of the *Upanishads* which teach the non-dual unity of Brahman at the expense of manifoldness (*Ch. U.*, VI.2.1; VII.25.2; *B.U.*, II.4.6; III.7.23; III.8.11; *M.U.*, II.2.11; *Īśā*, 7). Even the *Gītā* teaches the same in various passages (*B.G.*, VII.19; XIII.2.27). Shankara takes his stand on passages like the following:

> "In that all this has its self (Ātman, soul); it is the True, it is the
> "Self, Thou art that" (*Ch.U.*, VI.8.7)
> "The Self is all this" (*Ch.U.*, VII.25.2)
> "This everything, all is that Self" (*B.U.*, II.4.7)
> "Brahman alone is all this" (*Muṇḍ. U.*, II.2.11)
> "There is no diversity" (*B.U.*, IV.4.25)

Not only Shankara has selected certain passages to support his monism, but has argued in favour of it with a great deal of subtle arguments and has defended his thesis against all possible objections. With these observations we can deal with Shankara's philosophy.

Shankara's whole philosophy has been epitomized in one sentence: *Brahma satyam, jaganmithya jivo brahmaiva nā parah* i.e. Brahman alone is real, the world is illusory and the jīva is identical with Brahma. As the religious philosophy of Shankara is related more with Brahma and the jīva, so we shall pay our attention to these two topics without explaining much the illusoriness of the world. Let us take up the problem of Brahman first.

Brahman

The key-notion 'Brahman' has been derived from *bṛh* which means swelling or growing (towards the higher in man). It is really a symbol of the magical potency for attaining one's highest destiny, if an individual is being prepared for this ascent by the sacred and esoteric learning. It also may mean a collection of sacred and esoteric learning. It also may mean a collection of sacred prayers offered to gods at all times.[1]

The *Upanishads* have described Brahman, 'one without a second' as indescribable (*anirvacanīyam*) i.e. beyond any human category of thought or speech. Being unproduced, Brahman cannot be derived from any other pre-existing being (*Sat*), nor non-being (*asat*) (*Ch. U.*, VI.2.2), nor can be derived from anything less general (*Vs.*, III.2.9). This point has been further elaborated in the cosmological proof of theism (*Vs.*, I.1.5; I.4.22-23, 26, 27).

The most common way of speaking about Brahman is that it is *satyam, jñānam, ānandam*. To keep to the indescribable nature of B, it is mentioned in terms of double negatives i.e., B, is not *asat* (illusory or unreal), not *acit* (ignorance or insentient) and not *ānandam* or *dukkha* (suffering).[2] Why the negative way of Lord Buddha and Buddhism? Because negation implies affirmation, as Hegel has taught us. Shankara puts it thus:

[1]S.K. Belvalkar and R.D. Ranade, *History of Indian Philosophy*, pp. 346-47, 352.

[2]K.D. Bhattacharya, *A Modern Understanding of Advaita*, p. 41n.

> "Wherever we deny something unreal, we do so with reference to something real; the unreal snake, e.g., is negatived with reference to the real rope." (*Vs.*, III.2.23, p. 168).

By saying that Brahman is not *asat*, it is meant to say that it is most *sat*, not ajñānam implies that it is pure CS, and by saying it is not touched by suffering it is meant to emphasize that B, is unalloyed bliss. Hence, the negative way of describing Brahman simply means that B, is beyond the world of seeming things, beyond the thought and miseries of the finite individuals and beyond all human illusion. But the more about this in the sequel. It is to be noted here that existence (being, *sat*), pure consciousness (without having any object of anything and without itself being an object to itself) and bliss are not the attributes of Brahman. Brahman is *sat*, *cit* and *ananda*, and, all these are identical with B, itself. The key to the understanding of B, as Being, CS and Bliss is that it is *Atman*.

Atman is said to be derived from *av* (to blow) or *an* (to breathe), meaning that breath is of primary significance. It is also derived from *at* (to wander) which significantly refers to the doctrine of endless rebirths of a *Jivatma.*[1] That all that is and appears to human experience is Brahman, and, that Brahman is *Atman* has been thus elaborated.

This is *Atman*; 'That art thou, Śvetaketu' (*Ch. U.*, VI.8-16) has been repeated nine times by Uddalaka Aruni to his son Śvetaketu. This again is contained in the *mahāvākyas* '*Tattvamasi*' and '*Aham brahma*'. If B, is *Atman* then the most important characteristic of it is that it is consciousness. It is that which remains in the self-same manner in one's waking, dreaming and dreamless sleep. It is pure consciousness, without being the consciousness of any object. It remains the same, without any change in spite of its manifestations. It is that which makes individual knowers know, their objects.

> "Here the object of knowledge changes according as it is something past or something future or something present; but the knowing agent does not change, since his nature is eternal presence" (*Vs.*, II.3.7).

[1]Belvalkar and Ranade, op. cit., p. 357.

Here one can easily detect the adumbration of Kant's 'synthetic unity of apperception' and the eternal relating consciousness of T.H. Green which was raised to the ontological status of the Absolute. This CS, according to Shankara, is present in all acts of consciousness, but itself is not an object of any cognition (*B U.*, IV.4.18; *Vs.*, III.3.54; *Kena.*, V.11.4). It is the invariable witness, permanent in all transitory things, uniform, one, eternally unchanging and the self of everything (*Vs.*, I.1.4). Much later on in the *Siddhantabindu*, Madhusudan Sarasvati also writes that underlying the individual self as the doer and enjoyer of acts, there is the unchanging self which remains the witness of all changes.

> "Although, the means of knowledge, knowledge itself and the thing to be known may vary (at different times), the one who witnesses their existence and non-existence does not vary at all . . . ."[1]

Therefore, the essence of *Atman* is consciousness and not *self-consciousness* which is found in *cogito ergo sum,* and which was raised to the status of a key-concept in Hegelianism. In dreamless sleep, according to Advaitism, this Self is mere consciousness, without any object. Thus, this *Atman* is pure consciousness (*Vs.*, III.2-16-17, 22). This pure consciousness is not to be understood as self-consciousness (*Vs.*, III.2.16-17, 22). The reality of the *cit* cannot be denied without self-contradiction, according to Shankara:

> "For one cannot establish the Self in the case of anyone, because in itself it is already known. For the Self is not demonstrated by proof of itself. For it is that which brings into use all means of proof, such as perception and the like . . . ."[2]
>
> (*Vs.*, II.3.7)*

[1]Madhusudan Saraswati, *Siddhantabindu*, p. 56, notes.

[2]K.H. Potter, *Encyclopaedia of Indian Philosophies* (*EIP*), vol. III, *Upadeśa-sahasrī*, pp. 226, 232-35, 245-48, where this eternal seer has been called 'sākṣna'.

*The *Bhāmatī* puts it thus:

"And because of being the self of all, the existence of Brahman is well known. Everyone, verily, cognises the existence of himself; he does not cognise 'I do not exist'." (*The Bhāmatī catus-sutri*, tr. S.S. Suryanarayana Sastri, p. 110). Again,

"It is not possible to deny the self; for, even he who denies, even for him there is the selfhood" (Ibid., p. 206).

As consciousness in the Self cannot be denied without self-contradiction, so B, as *Atman* is CS and as such does exist. Of course, it would be meaningless to say that B, as consciousness does not exist. Nor *sat* and CS can be separated, because B, is non-dual.

Hence, it can be maintained that consciousness and being are one and the same as Brahman.

> "And if it finally should be said that existence is thought and thought existence and that the two do not exclude each other, we remark that in that case there is no reason for the doubt whether Brahman is that which is, or intelligence or both" (*Vs.*, III.2.21).

Similarly, it is said that B, is knowledge and that it is bliss (*Taitt. U.*, II.5, 7; *B.U.*, III.9.28).

> "Brahman is knowledge, is bliss".

Hence, B does not have CS, Being and Bliss as its attributes, but is CS, is Being and is Bliss. By way of summarising the main teachings of Shankara concerning Brahma we cannot down the following points.

In *V.*, III.2.7 Shankara quotes *B.U.*, IV.3.21; II.5.19; and in *Vs.*, III.2.16 he quotes to show that Brahman is completely undifferentiated without any inside or outside. It is like a mass of salt, without inside and outside. Hence, Brahman can be described by way of negation only. *Kaṭh.*, III.15 states that Brahman is soundless, formless, tasteless, odourless imperishable, without any beginning or end. Hence *Muṇḍ.*, III.1.8; *B.U.*, III.9.26 and *Taitt.*, II.9 describe It is incomprehensible, for It cannot be grasped by sight or by any sense organ or speech. Without attaining Brahma words along with the mind turn back (*Taitt.*, II.4.9). Thus, Shankara states that 'silence' is the only thing which can be maintained with regard to Brahma. He relates that Bāhva on being questioned about Brahman three times, keeping his silence all the time, at last uttered:

> "I am teaching you indeed, but you do not understand. Silent is that Self" (*Vs.*, III.2.17).

Hence we can say that Brahma is wholly incomprehensible, and, is beyond the known and unknown (*Kena.*, 1.3, quoted in *Vs.*, III.2. 17). Lastly Shankara subscribes, to *ajātivāda* and holds that Brahma is beyond causality (*Vs.*, III.2.30) and is absolutely unproduced man (*Vs.*, II.3.9) and unevolved (*Vs.*, III.2.23).

Though utterly incomprehensible and undifferentiated, yet Brahman is all this world, and by knowing this Brahman everything else can be known (*B.U.*, II.4.5; IV.5.6; *Muṇḍ.*, I.1.3). How?

> "Just as, my dear, by one piece of clay everything made of clay is known . . . . by one copper ornament everything made of copper may be known . . . . by one nail-scissors everything made of iron is known . . . . the modification is merely a verbal distinction, a name . . . .' (*Ch. U.*, VI.1.4-6).

In the same way by knowing Brahman all this world is known. The *Chāndogya* further elaborates this by stating that which is in the sun and the moon and in all this is the same as the *Atman* within the human heart.

> "That which is the finest essence—this whole world has that as its soul. That is Reality. That is Atman. That art thou, Śvetaketu" (VI.8.16).

Again, the *Śvetāśvatara* states the same thing:

> "As oil in sesame seeds, as butter in cream,
> As water in river-beds . . . .
> So is the Soul (Atman) apprehended in one's own soul,
> If one looks for Him with true austerity,
> . . . .
> This is Brahman, the highest mystic doctrine" (I.15-16).

Hence by knowing one's own Self, one can know Brahman. Thus the famous saying of the *Bṛhadāraṇyaka* is:

> ". . . . it is the soul that should be seen, that should be hearkened to, that should be thought on, that should be pondered on . . . ." (*B.U.*, II.4.5).

Therefore, now the problem has been pin-pointed. For knowing

Brahman, one should know one's own real Self. As such we have to ascertain the nature of the individual self before understanding the identity of jīva and Brahma.

How can Brahman be known through one's *Atman*? Of course, Brahman cannot be known in the ordinary sense of the term, for we have already seen that Brahman is incomprehensible. But what is important to know is that a jīva is identical with Brahman, and this is a matter of realisation. Hence, one has to know as to why this identity is not perceived and by knowing this secret one can realise one's identity with Brahman. The *why* of the situation is explained through the doctrine of māyā and the realisation of this identity is effected through the pathway of liberation. But before proceeding further both the identity formula and the relationship between the jīva and Brahma have to be explained. But without knowing the nature of jiva, the above-mentioned two issues cannot be explained.

The Nature of the Jīva

Avidya is the limitative adjunct of the jīva which prevents him from realizing his real nature of being Brahman himself. This *avidya* creates desire in him for the well-being of his body and for pleasure and aversion from pain (*Vs.*, I.3.2). Under the influence of *avidya*, the jīva accepts the seeming reality of names and forms, maintains the duality of subject and object and the plurality of EW (*Vs.*, I.3.19; II I.31). Due to *avidya*, the jīva regard himself as an agent of action and enjoyer of his deeds. *Upādhis* which serve as the principle of individuation are the following (*Vs.*, I.4.1; II.3.15; II.4.1-19).[1]

1. The Body.
2. *Karma-āsraya* with changes with every new birth.
3. Inseparable from jiva, though destructible by *Jñāna*.
   (a) The subtle body which may also be called the seed body, pertaining to rebirths.
   (b) The life-organs, called *prāṇas*,
   (c) Pertaining to conscious life consisting of five organs of sensing, five organs of action, and,
   (d) *Manas*.

[1]Paul Deussen, *The System of the Vedanta*, pp. 304, 325-26.

Manas is the central organ and is interchangeably used as *antaḥkaraṇa* (the inner organ).

From the above-mentioned characteristics of a jiva, it is clear that intellectual activities and will do not form part of the real nature of the jiva. Will and intellect are passible only when the jiva functions through the physical apparatus mentioned above.

Ahaṁkāra

Ahaṁkāra, also at times called *Buddhi*, is the most important *upādhi* of an individual.

> ". . . . the ahaṁkāra is a particular transformation (evolute) resulting from its having Parameshvara as substratum; it (viz. ahaṁkāra) is the substratum of *Jñānashakti* (thought-energy) and *Kriyashakti* (kinetic-energy); it is the sole basis of agency and enjoyment (i.e., it gives rise to the notion of doer and enjoyer); it is a light generated by its association with the unchanging intelligence (*Caitanya*)."[1]

In other words, the supreme consciousness in the jīva is particularised by the inner organ (*antaḥkaraṇa*) which coming in contact with an object manifests it. *Siddhantabindu* of Madhusudan also maintains that *antaḥkaraṇa* (inner organ) residing in the body and pervading it throughout, goes out of the body through an external organ e.g., the eye, assumes the forms of those individual objects, just as the molten copper assumes the form of the mould into which it is cast. This change in the inner organ assuming the form of the object cognised is known as *Vṛtti*.[2] When, for example, the eye comes in contact with a chair in space, then *Vṛtti* assumes the form of the chair.

In every case of perception, the absolute *cit* as the witness is at the basis of any instance of cognition. T.M.P. Mahadevan has taken a beautiful example to illustrate the place of the supreme *cit* in relation to the internal organ in a perceptual situation. Suppose that there is room fitted with mirrors to reflect the light of the sun as soon as the sun-rays are allowed to enter the room. The objects of the room can be perceived only in the reflected light

[1]Padmapada, *Pañcapādikā*, pp. 67-68, Gaekwad Oriental Series no. 197, specially Varnaka I, pp. 26, 96.

[2]Madhusudan Saraswati, *Siddhantabindu*, pp. 105, 219-20, 235, 265.

from the mirrors. Now the mirrors have been likened to *antaḥkaraṇa* in relation to the sun which stands for Brahman or *cit*. Hence, in every case of perception, *cit* is the real light which illuminates every perceptual object. But this *cit* works only through the reflected light of the internal organ called *antaḥkaraṇa*.[1]

According to Prof. Mahadevan, there are two distinct processes involved in perception. For instance, it is known that there is a pot, and, in the second phase it is noted "I know this 'pot'." In the first phase the cognition of the pot shows the importance of the reflected light (*ābhāsa*) in the *antaḥkaraṇa* and the second phase showing the importance of 'I' is said to be due to *cit* alone. But even the reflected light is not possible without *cit*. Thus Brahman is the real source of every illumination or cognition.[2]

In every case of perception, the *Vṛtti* (the psychosis as the result of the changed state of the internal organ) goes out to the external object through the pathway of the senses, and by assuming the form of the object reveals it. But *antaḥkaraṇa* is a product of *avidya*, and cannot help creating the illusory distinction of individual souls and empirical objects located in space, time etc. Perception only temporarily and very partially breaks up the veil concerning the objects. However, in every case of perception of knowledge in general, it is the supreme consciousness which is the real witness (Sākṣi) through *antaḥkaraṇa*. *Antaḥkaraṇa* through *Vṛtti* lights up the object, but even veridical perception is really the product of nescience. If *Vṛtti* be inappropriate, then illusion of the type of snake-rope and silver-conchshell will arise. The same *antaḥkaraṇa* in the state of doubt is called *manas*, with regard to knowledge proper is called *Buddhi*, and is called *Citta* in acts of remembering. *Ahaṁkara*, therefore, is that *Vṛtti* of *antaḥkaraṇa* which is the product of *avidya* and is characterized by *Jñāna* and *Kriyashakti*. In the state of dream, senses become inactive, but *manas* continues to function (*Vs*., III.2. 1-6). However in dreamless sleep, the *antaḥkaraṇa* and *ahaṁkāra* remain submerged in nescience: here only the witnessing self and nescience along with the past impressions (*saṁskāra*) alone continue to work. On waking, this *antaḥkaraṇa* begins to work and by being associated with nescience has the knowledge 'Oh': I did not know anything.[3]

[1]T.M.P. Mahadevan, *The Philosophy of Advaita*, p. 21.
[2]Ibid., p. 22.
[3]K.H. Potter, *EIP*, *Ch. U.B.*, p. 265; *AUB.*, p. 276.

Thus, the jīva as an individual *Atman* is not Brahman. But the scripture teaches also the identity of the jīva and Brahman. The *Chāndogya* repeats this identity nine times:

"That art thou, Śvetaketu" (VI.8.16).

We have now to explain and illustrate this relationship between a jīva and Brahman so that the identity statement be clearly grasped.

Jīva and Brahma

As individual is nothing but Brahma, but his nature remains concealed in a jīva because of his *avidya.*[1] In other words, the avidyaic adjuncts to which reference has already been made, make B, reflected as so many jīvas, or, by being limited by his *upādhis*, the jīva appears to be different from Brahma. Shankara described individuality as 'mere name and form' and this 'name and form' is like the foam, or waves of the sea, which do not constitute the essence of a jīva which is identical with Brahma (*Vs.*, II.1.13, 14). Shankara himself refers to three kinds of relation between a jīva and B, and, which have given rise to *ābhāsavāda* (semblance theory), *pratibimbavāda* (reflection theory) and *avacchedavāda* (limitation theory). At one place, Shankara refers to both reflection theory and limitation theory:

> "Just as the light of the sun or the moon which pervades the entire space becomes straight or bent as it were when the limiting adjuncts with which it is in contact, such as a finger, for instance, are straight or bent, but does not really become so and just as the ether, although imagined to move as it were when jars are moved, does not really move; and as the sun does not tremble, although its image trembles when you shake the cup filled with water in which the sun's light is reflected. . . ."
>
> (*Vs.*, II.3.46; also see III.2.25)

So in terms of these similes, Shankara states at the vicissitudes in the life of a jīva do not touch B. In the same manner, Shankara clearly states the reflection theory in *Vs.*, II.3.50; III.2.10, 20.

[1]Shankara rejects the notion that jīvas are *parts*, like so many sparks of one fire, K.H. Potter, *EIP*, *BUB*., p. 190.

> "The reflected image of the sun dilates when the surface of the water expands, it contracts when the water is agitated . . . . It thus participates in all the attributes and conditions of the water; while the real sun remains all the time the same".
>
> (*Vs.*, III.2.20)

In the same way B, appears to participate illusorily in the actions and feelings of the jīvas. Thus, Shankara accepts this comparison of B, to the sun reflected in water.

Again, Shankara along with reflection view, advances limitation theory in *Vs.*, II.1.13 and II.3.46. For Shankara the relation between B, and the jīvas is analogous to the sea and waves. He refers to it thus :

> ". . . . Just as the universal ether is divided by its contact with jars and other limiting adjuncts, so the upadhis serve as the limiting adjuncts" (*Vs.*, II.1.13).

Again,

> "That same soul (Brahma), on the other hand, which exists in all bodies, if considered apart from limiting adjuncts, is nothing else but the highest Self. Just as the spaces within jars, if considered apart from their limiting conditions, are merged in universal space, so the individual soul also is incontestably that which is denoted as the abode of heaven and earth, since it (the jiva) cannot really be separate from the highest Self". (*Vs.*, I.3.7).

What was stated by Shankara with regard to the relationship between jīvas and B, has been sought to be elucidated by *ābhāsavāda*, *pratibimbavāda* and *avacchedavāda*. All these theories may vary in detail, but they all seek to show non-difference of the jīva with Brahman,

> "For on the doctrine of the non-difference of the individual soul and the highest Self the Vedanta texts insist again and again" (*Vs.*, III.2.25).

In the light of the last contention, we can say that a jīva is a complex of Self and non-Self. All experiences of the ego, either in waking or dreaming are ultimately illusory. But the essential self underlying the changing experiences of the ego is the supreme *cit*. It is this *cit* which serves as the illuminating activity limited by the avidyaic cover. But even then this *cit* in this *bliss-sat* is best experienced in *suṣupti* and better still in the state of *turiya*. Keeping these two aspects of the jiva, it can be said to have a twofold mode of existence, substantial (*atma-rupa* or *svarupa* self) and adjectival (or, *sambandhi* self.) The underlying permanent (*Kuṭastha*) self remains the same in spite of changes. But the seeming changes follow from his relations with other things.

> "Devadatta although being one only forms the object of many different names and notions as he is considered in himself or in his relation to others; thus he is thought and spoken of as man, Brahmana, learned in the Vedas, generous etc.,......" (*Vs*., II.2.17).

The changing states of a jīva are like the foams, waves of the ocean which in no way affect the essential nature of the ocean.

Now according to *ābhāsavāda* (Semblance theory) of Sureshvara, the supreme Self has the semblance with the Brahma contained in certain limiting agents. This emphasizes the unreality of EW and individuality. This theory verges on *pratibimbavāda* (Reflection theory), according to which the Self is reflected as so many jīvas in the same way in which one moon when reflected in water appears to be many. Further, it has been held that B, reflected in māyā is felt as Īshvara, and, this Īshvara is further reflected in the avidyaic *antaḥkaraṇa* in a jiva. However, both *bimb* and *pratibimba* (i.e., Īshvara and jīva respectively) are identical. It is the *bhedadṛṣṭi* form of nescience which prevents the seeing of their identity. As against this reflection theory, *ābhāsavāda* maintains that EW and the plurality of jivas are non-existent at all times, and, Brahman, and EW and jīvas in the state of nescience cannot be identical (*abhinna*). EW is *asat* in *Sat* B, according to *vivartavāda*. EW and jīvas have their substratun *in* B, but cannot be said to be identical with B. Hence, *ābhāsavāda* holding on to *vivartavāda* as against *pariṇāmavāda*, emphasizes the unreality of the manifold.

Again, *ābhāsavāda* differs from limitation theory inasmuch as *avacchedavāda* states that B, like all-pervading *akasha* can be conditioned by adjuncts. Of course, the simile must not be pushed too far, for B, is not a material entity which can be limited like *akasha.* However, *avacchedavāda* seeks to show the relation of non-difference between B, and the jīvas, as against *ābhāsavāda* and *pratibimbavāda* which seek to emphasize the unreality of the manifold, and, the eternal, unchangeable purity and infinitude of B. Thus, the theories are really complementary for all of them keep to the same fundamental advaitic monism of Shankara.

The nature of a jīva shows that the jīva is a product of avidya and so is the world. Hence, we have now to explain the nature of avidya, better known as māyā.

MĀYĀVĀDA

The Origin of Māyāvāda

The *Upanishads* describe Brahman as unoriginated, eternal and changeless. But EW is constituted of changes. How can the only one, non-dual B, give rise to EW? According to Gauḍapāda, *Sat, Asat* and *Sadasat* cannot be regarded either as self-caused or caused by anything different from them (*MK.*, IV: 22). It is also contended that B, cannot be the cause of EW, in any extant sense of the term 'cause'. However, the *Upanishads* do talk of creation of EW as so many sparks from the one fire called Brahman. How are the two accounts be reconciled?

For Shankara, EW has been superimposed on the changeless B, in the same way in which the snake is superimposed on its underlying substratum called the rope. How is this superimposition effected? According to Shankara, it is *ajñāna* by which the jīvas experience multiplicity in the place of unity. Hence, the doctrine of *ajñāna.*

Shankara himself has not fully faced the problems which have besetted māyāvāda from the very beginning. He has not further analysed the notion of *ajñāna* into māyā, avidya and adhyāsa. In post-Shankara Advaitism these terms with their ramifications have assumed many subtle distinctions and discussions. We shall not go into all the scholastic debates and discussions, but shall have to refer to some of them in order to appreciate the subtleties of Advaitic thought. In later post-Shankara Advaitism the terms māyā, avidya and adhyāsa (superimposition) have been extensively used and even the doctrine of Shankara has come to be known as māyāvāda. Hence, the term 'māyā', 'avidya' etc. have to be used and explained.

RV., CLXXVII speaks of 'an Asura's magic might'. But in general both Indra and Varuṇa are said to be invested with māyā. According to H.D. Griswold[1] the term 'maya' has been used at least four times concerning Varuṇa (*RV.*, V.85.5, 6; VIII.41.3, 8) in the sense of 'occult powers' and magic wiles (VIII.41.8). In the same way, the term 'māyā' occurs thirty times at least in Indra hymns.

> "The world '*maya*' signifies occult, incomprehensible, superhuman powers, (following the interpretation given by H. Oldenberg) and so easily passes into the meanings, trick, magic, illusion, etc."[2]

Indra is credited to assume changes in his bodily forms by means of his māyā (*RV.*, III.53.8; VI.47.18). But quite obviously the *Ṛgvedic* māyā is quite different in meaning which is attached to Shankara's use of *ajñāna*, *avidya* and *adhyāsa*. But what about the *Upanishads* for which Shankara had the greatest respect, and for whose interpretation he used his māyāvāda?

George Thibaut very cautiously remarks that the māyā-doctrine may be implicit in the *Upanishads*, but explicitly this doctrine is not found in the *Upanishads*, except in the later *Upanishads* like *Maitri* and *Śvetāśvatara* (*SBE*, vol. XXXIV, p. cxvii and footnote). *B.U.*, II.5, 19 quotes *RV.*, VI.47.18 in which the term 'māyā' occurs with regard to Indra. But if all the *Upanishads*, including the later ones be included, then, according to Dr. Ramamurti Sharma,[3] the term 'māyā' has been used 25 times in them, the term 'māyā' has been used in the sense of 'occult power' (*BU.*, II.5.19) as trickery (*P.U.*, I.16), and *Śvet. U.*, IV.9, 10 describes Nature as an illusion and the mighty Lord as the illusion maker. Even Shankara appears to have used 'māyā' as 'magical potency' by which the Lord has created the world (*Vs.*, II.1.9). Apart from the *Upanishads*, according to Dr. R. Sharma, the *Gītā* has used the

[1] H.D. Griswold, *The Religion of Ṛgveda*, p. 137.
[2] Ibid , p. 186, 186n.
[3] Ramamurti Sharma, *Advaita Vedanta*, p. 161.

term 40 times (largely as the creative power as Shakti)[1] and Brahma-sutra only once. Hence, the māyā-doctrine cannot be ascribed to the *prasthana traya* which is the basis of Shankara's māyāvāda. The very fact that Rāmānuja and his followers do not discern the māyā-doctrine is enough to show that māyāvāda is not explicitly stated in the *prasthana traya.* Of course, Gauḍapāda uses 'māyā' in Shankara's sense, 25 times and Gauḍapāda himself was indebted to *Vijñānavāda* for his doctrine of illusion. Hence, Shankara is directly indebted to his grand-guru Gauḍapāda and indirectly to *Vijñānavāda.* But from this absence of explicit māyāvāda, it does not follow that the germ of illusionism is not present in the *Upanishads.*[2]

Īśā U., 15 tells us that the Truth is veiled, which simply means that EW is false, *BU.*, IV.4.19 states.

> "He gets death after death, who perceives here seeming diversity."

In the same manner, the famous prayer of the *Bṛhadāraṇyaka* contains the following:

> "From the unreal lead to the real:
> From darkness lead to light" (*BU.*, I.3.28)

Ch. U., VIII.3.2 speaks of the persons who are carried away astray by what is false, and, *Ch. U.*, VI.3.2.3 speaks about the separating 'out name and form'. *Kaṭh. U.*, II.4 makes a distinction between *vidya* and *avidya*, and, II.5 (also *Muṇḍ. U.*, I.2.8) tells us that people abiding in the midst of ignorance go around deluded. Similarly, *Muṇḍ. U.*, II.1.10 prays to the Supreme Person to 'cut asunder the knot of ignorance'.

In short, the *Upanishads* describe the diversity and other allurements of EW as false, due to blinding *avidya* and delusion in one's

[1]Prof. T.G. Mainkar in his book *A Comparative Study of the Commentaries on the Bhagavadgītā*, p. 7, mentions that 'māyā' may be said to be power or Shakti of 'the Lord Kṛṣṇa'. Then, again, Mainkar denies that *Bhagavadgītā* teaches the doctrine of illusionism. According to him, five clear passages, containing the term 'māyā' (IV: 6; VII: 14-15, 25; XVIII: 61) do not even hint at the doctrine of illusionism, p. 10, ibid.

[2]R.D. Ranade, *The Constructive Survey of Upanishadic Philosophy*, pp. 224-28.

heart. This *avidya,* delusion concerning diversity can easily be treated as Illusion, specially if one has to uphold the oneness, unchangeableness, non-origination of Brahman. Shankara chooses to interpret the important trend of monism in the *Upanishads* on the basis of illusionism, according to the inspiring vision contained in Gauḍapāda's *Māṇḍūkya-Kārikā.* For this reason 'diversity' (*nānātva*) and falsity (*anṛta*) have been interpreted as illusory in the interest of upholding the non-dual reality of Brahman.

In fairness to Shankara it has to be pointed out here that Shankara uses the term *ajñāna* as a technical term to connote illusionism. Roughly the frequency of *ajñāna* and *māyā* is ten to two, at least in *Vs.* Even when Shankara uses the term 'Māyā', he uses it in various senses, viz., *deception* (*Vs.*, II.3-6), as *magic* (*Vs.*, I.1.17; I.3.19; II.1.9, 21, 28-29), as *marvellous power* (*Vs.*, I.1.20; I.4.3; II.1.37; II.2.4; 2.7). These instances would show that for Shankara, *ajñāna* was a really technical term and not *māyā.*[1] If the critics of Shankara only paid attention to this fact, then they would have desisted from much fruitless discussion. Thus, we now discuss this nature of nescience, though we cannot give up the term 'māyāvāda' because of its currency in relation to Advaitism.

The Nature of Nescience (*Ajñāna*)

Ajñāna is that mysterious force which generates the whole empirical world consisting of manifold names and forms, comprising Īshvara, jīva, the ordered external world, and even gods and the heaven. Hence, nescience is the principle of individuation which makes the undifferentiated Brahman appear as many. It not only conceals the reality, but also distorts it. It is beginningless (*anādi*) but has an end (*sānta*) because it disappears which the dawning of B-realisation. It is an unbiquitous force for the jīvas and is manifested in such experience is 'Oh: I do not know what you say', or, on awakening from deep sleep we say 'I do not know anything during my sleep'. Hence, Sriharṣa says that it is nescience which produces the indefinite experience of objects. It is found both in its primary and secondary forms. In Buddhism this is known as *tathya Samvṛti* (primary nescience) and *mithyā samvṛti* (secondary nescience). Ordinary snake-rope or conch-silver illusions come under secondary nescience. But the whole empirical world of trans-indivi-

[1]P. Hacker and S. Mayeda also hold that the term *avidya* is more Shankarite than *māyā* (K.H. Potter, *EIP*, p. 115).

dualistic construction including science comes under primary nescience. If EW is an appearance, then ordinary illusions may be called appearances of appearance, distorted through sense-organs, distance and other auxiliary forces. In comparison with the *pāramārthika* or Supreme reality, EW is as 'illusory as the magic-show by a juggler' (exactly as Gauḍapāda describes this). But this EW caused by nescience is much more real than dreams, for it is ordered and runs regularly according to fixed laws. It is also collectively verified by our veridical perception (*Vs.*, I.3.30). As Shankara puts it:

> ". . . . as long as true knowledge does not present itself, there is no reason why the ordinary course of secular and religious activity should not hold on undisturbed" (*Vs.*, II.1.14).

Nescience cannot be said to be a purely negative force. On the contrary, it is a positive force since it is generative of the whole gamut of EW. It is neither *sat* nor *asat*. It is not sat, because it gets dissolved when B-realisation dawns. It is not wholly *asat* because of the veridical perception of trans-individualistic and inter-subjective discourse. If *ajñāna* were really *sat*, then it would never disappear, and, if it were unreal then it would not conceal and distort the reality. Hence, it has been described as *sadasad-vilakṣaṇa* (i.e., *anirvacanīya* or indescribable). Naturally the question will arise, whence is this nescience and what is its locus?

No Indian system interested in soteriological investigation has attempted at the genesis of nescience. It has been stated as beginningless. What is the meaning of 'beginningless'? Is it within the order of time or outside the order of time? If it is outside the series of time, then it may mean something like the eternal ideas of Plato or *cit* or *ālayavijñāna.* However, it cannot be so, since nescience is not absolutely real. Then, it may mean something like mathematical eternity which is born of linguistic convention e.g., $2 + 2 = 4$. But this linguistic convention cannot account for the metaphysical verity which Advaitism seeks to establish. If, however, beginningless simply means that which *endures* for ever, then too it cannot be true of Advaitism, since it does come to an end with the dawning of *B-jñāna.* Of course, Sāṃkhya does admit that nescience comes into being with the infatuation of the spirit coming in contact with Prakṛti. Thus, nescience of an individual has a beginning even when it cannot be dated. But this view cannot be acceptable to an advaitin. First, because Sāṃkhya explanation is based on the dualism of *Puruṣa* and *Prakṛti*, which dualism is rejected by Shankara. Secondly, this doctrine of an individual infatuation may have a history, but for the cosmic nescience there can be no history. And the Advaitism of Shankara is interested in cosmic nescience. Is the concept of nescience plainly unintelligible and inconsistent, as S.N. Dasgupta[1] would say? Paul Deussen appears to have the same opinion too.[2]

According to Paul Deussen, Shankara suggests that nescience is beginningless, and, jivas are born with *avidya*. Does this *avidya* follow from previous births? Paul Deussen remarks:

> "Avidya cannot properly be a result of *Samsara*, for on the contrary reverse is the case and the whole of *Samsara* depends on avidya."[3]

Naturally, the origin of Saṃsāra, even if not in terms of time-series, at least ontologically has to be traced to Brahman.[4] True, jīvas view reality in a warped way because of their adjuncts (*upādhis*). But *upādhis* ultimately have to be accounted by nescience:

> "Avidya alone is the cause of the origin of the *upadhis*. . . .and is the cause of their persistence so far as the essence of *avidya* is non-discrimination of Brahman from the *upadhis* . . . ."[5]

But quite obviously, as B, is quality-less (both internal and external) and as B, remains unaffected by *upādhis*, so B, can have no relationship with nescience. Hence, the beginningless nescience cannot have its locus either in the jīvas (as against the *jivashrita* view of nescience), or in Brahman (as against the *Brahma-ashrita* view of nescience). Once more we find that nescience is wholly inexplicable.

The doctrine of nescience is a postulate for Shankara, and, its utility lies in effecting liberation. Once liberation has been achieved, then this achievement not only is said to verify the postulate, but

[1]S.N. Dasgupta, *A History of Indian Philosophy*, vol. II, p. 13.
[2]Paul Deussen, *The System of the Vedanta*, p. 303.
[3]Ibid., p. 303.
[4]S.N. Dasgupta, *A History of Indian Philosophy*, vol. II, p. 35.
[5]Paul Deussen, *The System of the Vedanta*, p. 303.

also at the same time may be said to constitute its 'truth'. The preoccupation of Indian thought is purely diagnostic and therapeutic. It seeks release from worldly entanglement. It is the urgency of soteriological interest which throttles any further metaphysical enquiry about the origin of nescience. This is an easily discernible (motive) motif of *Upanishads*. Buddhism went a step ahead, and, declared metaphysical inquisitiveness a heresy. Further, the therapeutic effect of Yogic practice demonstrated to the serious seekers the plausibility of reaching a state of objectless and pure consciousness. Even apart from this Yogic state of *turiya*, the common experience of deep sleep had convinced the thinker of the possibility of reaching a state of pure consciousness. Hence, both the Mahayanist Buddhism and Shankarite Advaitism have their efforts concentrated in building a philosophical edifice of pure consciousness. For Buddhism this is called Shūnyavāda which it denies to be nihilism, and, for Shankara, it is a state of undifferentiated CS, without being parted by any relation, whether internal or external. The reality of pure and objectless consciousness is already clear from Yājñavalkya and Maitreyi *saṃvāda* (dialogue). Yājñavalkya declares that B is consciousness itself, without any object whatsoever (*Vijñāna-ghana*). A man on obtaining knowledge enters into this infinite mass of consciousness, after his death.

> " 'After death there is no consciousness'
> Thus spoke Yajñavalkya"

Maitreyi took this statement as tantamount to nihilism, and uttered in alarm.

> "Herein, indeed, you have bewildered me, Sir—in saying 'After death there is no consciousness'."

Yājñavalkya hastens to correct the misunderstanding and declares that the final state is consciousness without any quality and literally indescribable (*BU.*, II.4. 13-14).

Hence, the Indian thinkers felt sure of the state of release. Why should have they occupied themselves with unnecessary problem of the genesis of nescience?

For us, the whole structure of Shankara's Advaitism stands on the root-metaphor of dreamless sleep or *turiya* state. The dialectic on which it is based in terms of indescribable nescience casts a cloud of unintelligibility. Thus, the foundation and even the logic of nescience provide a shaky foundation of advaitic structure. Is it a great blemish? Yes, but the value of a metaphysics is to be judged not in terms of its logic and content, but in terms of the vision it provides for the life as a whole. But this kind of evaluation of Advaitism will be taken up in its proper place.

Even if it be granted that māyā is beginningless even though it has an end, the question still remains, 'what is the locus of this māyā'? The problem is ticklish. At the outset we have to state that māyā has its seat in the jiva which causes a *mithyadṛṣṭi* in him. As there can be nothing real beside Brahman so the target or screen on which this *dṛṣṭi* projects illusory plurality is Brahman. But the screen remains unaffected by what is projected on it.

The Locus of Māyā

The doctrine of māyā is not very strong in the earlier *Upanishads*. Hence, they do not say anything about the seat of māyā. Even Gauḍapāda has not clarified the issue. Is māyā in Brahman or is its seat in the jivas? Gauḍapāda mentions both B, and the jīvas as the seat of *avidya*. Shankara certainly was aware of the problem, but he did not decide either in favour of *Brahmāshritavāda* or *Jivāshritavāda*. He mentions both the views. As noted earlier, Shankara mentions in his commentary on *Śvet. U.*, IV.9-10 and other passages in the *Gītā* that Īshvara creates the world by virtue of his māyā. As Īshvara and Brahman are very close, so this māyā of Īshvara may be said to belong to Brahman in a metaphorical sense (*Vs.*, IV.1.6). However, in *B.U.B.*, 1.4.10 Shankara more explicitly states that *avidya* has its substratum in Brahman.[1] In this context the objector holds that B, is not the cause of the superimposition of the attributes on Itself, nor is it the author of ignorance. Shankara replies:

> "Let it be so, Brahman is not the author of ignorance nor subject to error. But it is not admitted that there is any other conscious entity but Brahman which is the author of ignorance

[1]Shankara does maintain that Brahma is the seat of *avidya*. But he clarifies this point by further stating that Brahman has really no relation with *avidya*. Only through *avidya*, quite naturally in jīva that Brahman is seen to be the locus of *avidya* (K.H. Potter, *EIP*, pp. 468-69).

> or subject to error. Witness such Shruti texts as, 'There is no other knower but Him' (*BU.*, III.7.23), 'There is no other knower but this" (*BU.*, III.8.11).[1]

As against Brahman as the substratum of māyā, Shankara advances the other view too that the jīva is the locus of māyā (*Vs.*, I. 3.2., I.3.19, and I.4.3). However, Shankara's commentary on *BU.*, XIII.2 is most interesting. Here he points out that the question about the locus of māyā is irrelevant. Māyā cannot be in *cit.* The question can be answered if *avidya* is perceived and also the entity which has this *avidya.* The opponent states:

> "Why, it is I who have *avidya,* and I should try and get rid of it."

Reply: Then you know *avidya* and the Self, its possessor, ...[2] Shankara now points out that this knowledge of the locus of *avidya* is not possible. Why? Because the supreme knower (the Self) cannot be an object to itself.

> "It is not indeed possible for you to perceive your Self as related to *avidya,* at the same moment (that your Self cognises *avidya*); for, the cogniser (the Self) acts at the moment as the percipient of *avidya.* Neither can there be a (separate) cogniser of the relation between the cogniser (the Self) and *avidya,* nor a separate cognition of that (relation); for then you would commit the fallacy of *infinite regress* (*anavasthā*). If the relation between the cogniser (the Self) and the cognised could be cognised, another cogniser should be supposed to exist; then another cogniser of that cogniser; then another of that again, and so on; and thus the series would necessarily be endless."[3]

The conclusion is negative. Brahman, the cogniser is not at all tainted by nescience, misery and the like[4] i.e., B has no connection with *avidya.* As a matter of fact, Shankara holds that *avidya* inheres in the organ.

[1] *BUB.*, Eng. tr. by Madhavananda, p. 14n.
[2] *BGB.*, Eng. tr. by A. Mahadeva Shastri, p. 333.
[3] Ibid., p. 334.
[4] Ibid., pp. 329, 331, 332n.

> ". . . . non-perception, false perception, and doubt, as well as their cause, properly pertain to the instrument, to one or another sense organ, but not to Kshetrajña, the cogniser."[1]

Having briefly discussed the key-notions of Brahman, Jīva and Māyā, we are in a position now to deal with the religious philosophy of Shankara. No doubt the religious philosophy of Shankara is monistic, but theism too occupies an important place in it. Therefore now we shall attend to this aspect of Shankara's philosophy. We shall also discuss the status of theism in Shankara's philosophy in the light of the serious objections raised both by Deussen[2] and by S.N. Dasgupta,[3] in the sequel.

The Notion of God

Strictly speaking there is only one non-dual B, which underlies the actual and possible objects of experience, including the experiencing egos. This changeless, differenceless and impersonal self-luminous consciousness is the ultimate illumining Reality which underlies all the states of dreaming, waking and dreamless sleeping. As such it is the underlying ground of all kinds of knowledge, illusions and thoughts. B is the real stuff which appears as EW by virtue of cosmic ignorance called māyā. Māyā is the principle of diversifying B into EW of things and individuals. Though māyā is the illusory cause of EW, yet it accounts for the real-unreal inexplicable EW as relatively real and makes B appear as EW. However, māyā leaves B, untouched and unaffected by its diversifying agency. Māyā veils the essential nature of B, and makes B appear as EW of manifold objects and individual jīvas. Māyā in its turn is a positive force which is inexplicable and beginningless, though it has an end.

> "It is through identification with Brahman the sole existence that the illusory phenomena of the world are experienced as real or existent, and it is by the luminosity of Brahman the sole self-luminosity of consciousness . . . . that they are illumined and manifested."[4]

[1]*BGB.*, Eng. tr. by A. Mahadeva Shastri, pp. 323-24.
[2]Paul Deussen, *The System of the Vedanta*, p. 279.
[3]S.N. Dasgupta, A *History of Indian Philosophy*, vol. I, p. 477.
[4]M.K.V. Iyer, *Advaita Vedanta*, p. 34.

Hence, B, as illusorily conditioned by ignorance is both the material and efficient cause of EW. Of course, this causation is only apparent and not real. Thus, both the material and efficient cause of the world comes to be illusorily related to EW. This illusorily conditioned saguṇa Brahman called 'Īshvara' is not ultimate but only relative. Thus conditioned by māyā, Brahman comes to be known as a personal Being. This personal Īshvara as a self-conscious, self-determining, omnipotent, omniscient, infinite Being is only a pictorial representation of B, projected on the colourless canvas of pure *cit*. The entire empirical world proceeds from Him and in relation to EW, God remains both immanent and immensely transcendent to the whole world. The individual jīvas come from Him and remain utterly subordinate to Him. As a transcendent Being God remains changeless, beyond spatio-temporal existence. However, as a creative and immanental Being, He is pictured as eternally modifying Himself into EW with its manifoldness located in spatio-temporal frame. Māyā, as the power of God, has no existence apart from Him, and, so is non-different from Him. but God as a person owns and controls His māyā. Besides, māyā leaves God unaffected by its creation of EW. As such māyā remains unaffecting and quite distinct yet inseparable from God. This position of God can be thus summarised: God is the efficient cause of the world and His power in the form of māyā is the material cause of EW. However, God as a personal Being, conditioned by māyā is not the highest reality.

It is not very difficult to see as to why Shankara does not take Īshvara to be the highest reality. Of course, Shankara takes his stand on those Upanishadic passages which teach strict monism i.e., the doctrine of non-dual Brahman, without a second. Īshvara not only has māyā but also many other auspicious attributes. In this sense, the doctrine of qualified Īshvara does not go with the acceptance of Brahman as the only undifferentiated, impartite, nirguṇa Brahman. Apart from this general stand, Īshvara being both transcendent and immanent in the world, becomes a composite being, and, as such becomes sundered from within. Then again, Īshvara uses māyā and yet gets unaffected by it. How can the modes and changes brought about by māyā can leave Īshvara unaffected, if māyā really belongs to Him? Further, Īshvara is said to be a person, but the very nature of personality is that it persists in the midst of changes, but the structure of personality does not remain the same with varying changes. Besides, if Īshvara be real, then all His modifications will be equally real. But dreams, illusions and even waking experiences in play, jest and seriousness cannot be regarded as equally real. For these reasons, perhaps, Shankara regards Īshvara as only phenomenally real, though He stands highest in the hierarchy of phenomenal existences. With the dawning of the final *B-Jñāna*, Īshvara with His māyā and EW as His māyic creation gets dissolved.

Brahma and Īshvara

Brahman is apprehended in two forms; there is the nirguṇa Brahma which is free from all adjuncts and attributes, and is described as *Saccidānanda* (*sat, cit* and *ānanda*). Secondly, the same Brahma, reflected *in* and *by* māyā comes to be pictured as the creator of the whole multiplicity of names and forms (*Vs.*, I.1.11; II.1.14). Thus qualified by māyā, B is known as Īshvara and is an object of devotion (*Vs.*, I.1.11; I.3.13). As an object of devotion, Brahma becomes *saguṇa* or comes to be invested with certain qualities . . . .' such as consisting of mind and the rest . . . . which qualities depend on its connection with certain pure limiting adjuncts; then it is what we call lower Brahman' (*Vs.*, IV.3.9; also vide III.2. 21-22; III.3.12; IV.3.14-15).

Vācaspati, following Maṇḍana, regards the jīva as the *āśraya* of *avidya*, but the jīva is not the creator of the world. No doubt, *avidya* is in the jīva, but that is not within his control.

> "The control of *avidya* belongs not to me with my limited powers of knowing and acting, but to the omniscient and omnipotent Being."[1]

This view of Īshvara, having its roots in N.V. theism becomes very important in the theism of Rāmānuja. But let us continue Shankara's view of Īshvara. Īshvara is the one and only eternal creator of the world (*Vs.*, II.3.30) and remains both immanent and transcendent to the world (*RV.*, X.90.1; *Vs.*, I.2.2-3; II.1.27 where Shankara quotes *Ch. U.*, III.12.6). He creates the world of the jīvas in accordance with their karmas (*Vs.*, II.3.41-42). As such He is not responsible for the miseries of jīvas; for which their own demerites are responsible (*BUB.*, I.4.10).

[1]Introduction to *Bhāmatī*, p. xxxvi.

> "Hence the Lord, being bound by regards, cannot be reproached with inequality of dispensation and cruelty" (*Vs.*, II.1.34; also see *Vs.*, III.2.38-41).

His knowledge and agency do not require any bodily organs (*Vs.*, I.1.5; II.2.3-4), for He is omniscient and omnipotent. The Lord is without a body, because

> "all bodies exist only subsequently to the creation, and none previously to it" (*Vs.*, II.2.40).

Besides, having a body will make the Lord dependent on senses as is the case with transmigratory souls. This will make the Lord cease to be the Lord (*Vs.*, II.2.40). However, the Lord may assume a bodily form by His own māyā for the benefit of His worshippers (*Vs.*, I.1.20; also see II.2.4 where the Lord is said to perform any activity with His māyā).

But the Lord even when He assumes different bodily forms, is not affected by pleasure and pain (*Vs.*, I.1.11-12) and is not in any way affected by His own māyā (*Vs.*, III.2.9). In other words, the Lord controls His own māyā. This point is repeatedly maintained by Shankara in *BGB.*

> "Just as the glamour caused by a juggler (mayavin) does not obstruct his own knowledge" (*BGB.*, VIII.25; see also IV.6; V.14; IX.10).

The Lord out of His own māyā, with regards to karmas of the jīvas and Time, evolves the world of names and forms i.e., the world of individuated things (*Vs.*, II.1.14; II.4.28).

However, the Lord along with His māyā belongs to the phenomenal reality and may be taken to be the highest in the hierarchy of the phenomena beginning with plants and animals gradually rising to men, gods and higher gods like Vaishvānara and Hiraṇyagarbha (*Vs.*, I.3.30; I.1.11). All lordly powers of the gods have been derived from the Lord (*Vs.*, I.2.28) and in like manner the jīvas depend on the Lord (*Vs.*, IV.4.17). At times, Shankara describes the relation of the jīvas with Īshvara as one of master and servant (*Vs.*, II.3.43-53) which relationship has assumed a very great importance in the later *bhakti* cult of Rāmānuja and others.

the world does not fulfil any thing which is not already accomplished in the Lord, and, also in the sense that creation is spontaneous and effortless on the part of the Lord as behoves His real nature (*Vs.*, II.1.33).

Shankara makes a sharp distinction between Īshvara and Brahman and regards Īshvara as an appearance only, and, lower than Brahman. Īshvara is only for the purpose of worship and is a mere concession to ordinary mind (*BUB.*, VIII.1.1; *Vs.*, I.1.1, 20, 24, 31; I.2.14; III.2.14) according to Shankara. For this reason, Paul Deussen comments that the role of God as creator sinks into a secondary and purely instrumental one.[1]

Again, S.N. Dasgupta writes:

> "In the Vedanta system Ishvara has but little importance, for he is but a phenomenal being."[2]

And yet, Shankara also maintains very close relationship between Īshvara and Brahman.

> "As the lower Brahman is in proximity to the higher one, there is nothing unreasonable in word 'Brahman' being applied to the former (i.e., Ishvara) also" (*Vs.*, IV.3.90).

Further, for Shankara, qualified Brahman is fundamentally one with the unqualified Brahman (*Vs.*, III.3.39); in reality the personal Self and the highest Self are identical (*Vs.*, I.4.1).

We shall be in a better position to discuss this when we pass on to the topic of liberation. However, without discussing in detail we can jot down the following points in this controversy. Even according to Advaitism of Shankara, without Īshvara the empirical world, its existence with its fixed order cannot be explained. Again, 'Worship' is not possible without Īshvara, and, this worship of the lord is a powerful means of obtaining *B-jñāna.* As a matter of fact Shankara himself has composed a number of beautiful hymns in praise of the various Gods, even though he was himself a Vaiṣṇava. At least some of these points can be discerned in the so-called knowledge of Brahma and Īshvara, in the form of proofs.

[1]Paul Deussen, *The System of the Vedanta*, p. 279.
[2]S.N. Dasgupta, *A History of Indian Philosophy*, vol. I, p. 477.

Brahma-jñāna and Theistic Proofs

Brahman is beyond subject-object distinction and beyond the categories of thought. As such he is beyond empirical knowledge. How else are we to have at least some working knowledge of B? According to Shankara, even ordinary things such as gems, spells and herbs are difficult to know by means of reflection alone, unaided by instruments . . .

> "how much more impossible is it to conceive without the aid of scripture the true nature of Brahman with its powers unfathomable by thought"! (*Vs.*, II.1.27).[1]

Why much more unfathomable by thought?

> "For Brahman, as being devoid of form and so on, cannot become an object of perception; and as there are in its case no characteristic marks (on which conclusion, &c. might be based), inference also and the other means of proof do not apply to it; . . ." (*Vs.*, II.1.6; also see I.1.4).

Then how to have some knowledge of B, to start with?

> "It is to be known solely on the ground of holy tradition" (*Vs.*, II.1.6).

Padmapāda further explains this position of Shankara:

> "The nature of the Shastra is this, that it is explicative of things which are not cognised (by other pramaṇas)". (*Pañca-pādikā*, VII.1; VII.4).

Of course, reasoning by itself alone fails to have any knowledge of B, for reasoning ultimately depends on inference, and, inference

[1]According to *Bhāmatī*, Brahman cannot be known through perception or inference.

'Only through intuition and that only by gifted and disciplined souls, whose minds have been purified by scripture-ordained duties and concentrated on the scripture-taught reality' (Introduction, p. xiii).

Thus, the *Bhāmatī* does not improve upon the contention made by Shankara.

in turn rests on *Vyāpti*, and this *Vyāpti* ultimately depends on repeated perception. But, B, being formless admits of no perception of B. Besides, by taking recourse to reasoning alone, without the aid of scripture, one like the Bauddhas can reach atheism and not theism. Hence, at the starting point any working knowledge of B, is imparted by scripture alone. However, reasoning has been considered to be an aid in understanding what the scripture communicates (*Vs.*, I.1.2; I.1.4; II.1.4; II.1.6; II.1.27; also *Pañcapādikā*, V.5.16-17).

Shankara takes the help of reasoning to assist the human understanding in grasping the nature of B, according to the injunctions of *BU.*, II.4.5 (the Self is to be heard, should be thought and pondered on: see *Vs.*, I.1.2).

This is necessary for removing the mistaken notion of Brahman (*Vs.*, I.1.1, p. 9) and of God. Shankara rejects the Naiyāyika notion of God, according to which God is only an efficient cause of the world. On the whole, however, the enterprise of Shankara is theological since reasoning remains subordinate to the scripture and is used for elucidating and defending the scriptural statements. In contrast the Naiyāyikas mainly depend on reasoning and only in their later development refer to the scripture. However, Shankara clearly states that Brahman is not to be known through reasoning alone (*Vs.*, II.I.31; II.1.6).

In advancing the arguments for the existence of God, Shankara rejects the following alternatives in explaining the nature of the world:

> ". . . not either from a non-intelligent *pradhana* (prakṛti), or from atoms, or from non-being, or from a being subject to transmigration; nor, again, can it proceed from its own nature (i.e., spontaneously). . . ." (*Vs.*, I.1.2).

Ontological Proof

But Shankara has so stated the nature of B, that it can be maintained by the so-called ontological proof, noting all the while that this proof is only an auxiliary aid or what can be termed as persuasive reasoning only. Secondly this does not show that B, has any quality at all. Even Anselm's Ontological proof is at most persuasive and only seeks to prove the bare Being or *sat* of God. Other proofs pertain to qualified Brahma or Īshvara.

According to Shankara, *B-Jñāna* is not an acquired knowledge by means of instruments of valid knowledge, for any knowledge which is acquired is open to dissolution. Hence, *B-Jñāna* is self-established.

> "But the Self, as being the abode of the energy that acts through the means of right knowledge, is itself established previously to that energy. And to refute such a self-established entity is impossible. An adventitious thing, indeed, may be refuted, but not that which is the essential nature (of him who attempts the refutation); for it is the essential nature of him who refutes" (*Vs.*, II.3.7).

In other words, the refuting intellect and the refuted CS, are one and the same, and, as such in the very moment of refuting B, ultimately it gets established. According to Shankara, Brahman is the underlying consciousness of perceiving, thinking and reasoning of any jīva whatsoever. Hence, *cit* by its very nature is absolutely *sat*, and, cannot be conceived to be non-existing at any moment *Sarvadā-vartamāna-svabhāvaṁ* (*Vs.*, II.3.7).

Here in the passage *cit*, by its very nature is said to be absolutely *sat* which clearly means that essence or idea implies God's existence. And this is the nerve of the ontological argument for the existence of God. Further, in Anselm's proof there is an axiological nuance in holding that a Being greater than whom nothing exists. Similarly Shankara also tries to prove the existence of God from His greatness.

> "For if we consider the derivation of the world 'Brahman', from the root *bṛh*, 'to be great', we at once understand that eternal purity, and so on, belong to Brahman" (*Vs.*, I.1.1).

> "Moreover the existence of Brahman is known on the ground of its being the Self of every one. For every one is conscious of the existence of (his) Self, and never thinks 'I am not'. If the existence of the Self were not known, every one would think 'I am not'. And this Self (of whose existence all are conscious inasmuch as he perceives, remembers etc.) is Brahman" (*Vs.*, I.1).

The latter part will remind one of John Caird's ontological argument. We must also not forget that Yahwe declared himself 'I am that I am' i.e., never to be conceived to be non-existing (*Exo.* 3.14).

But every student of religious philosophy knows that the ontological argument at most shows *that* there is God, but not *what* He is. Yet the what i.e., the qualified nature of Īshvara alone is worthy of worship. Hence, Shankara advances what can be called cosmological and teleological arguments for the existence of Īshvara. Once more we have to remember that these proofs are mere pleas, explicating the scriptural teaching with regard to Īshvara.

Cosmological Argument

Cosmological argument is based either on causal nexus, or, on the contingency of things in the world. Strictly speaking, taking our stand on *Vivartavāda*, and, Brahmāshrita māyā, this cosmological argument will be said to be based on contingency, because ultimately only Brahman is the necessary substratum of the world, jīva and even of Īshvara. But Shankara has not made any distinction between causal and contingency arguments.

Here Shankara tries to show that the world depends on Īshvara and secondly, EW cannot be conceived to be self-regulative (*Vs.*, I. 1.2).

Senses inform us about the objects, but mind is superior to both inasmuch as both of them depend on mind.

> "The intellect (buddhi) is higher than mind, since the objects of enjoyment are conveyed to the soul by means of the intellect. Higher than the intellect is the great Self which was represented as the Lord of the chariot . . . . ".

Again, a little earlier in the same passage, Shankara states:

> ". . . . the great Self is beyond the intellect, beyond the great (Mahat of Samkhya and the *Gītā*) there is the Undeveloped, beyond the undeveloped there is nothing (i.e., the nirguṇa Brahma). . . . this is the goal, the highest road" (*Vs.*, I.4.I).[1]

Hence, Īshvara is the ground of EW and the jīvas in the first instance and Brahman is the final substratum of everything.

Further, the Lord arranges the order and system of the sun and moon and of other things at the beginning of every Kalpa. But the

[1]Here one is reminded of Ludwig Wittgenstein.

order of the world in the whole hierarchy of gods, men and animals continues to be the same through all successive creations of the beginningless *saṁsāra*. The cause of this order cannot be due to anything else except the Lord. No material things can be the cause, for being inert they cannot give rise to anything, just as clay without any intelligent creator cannot give rise to pots (*Vs.*, I.1.5). In the same way, men, gods and not even Hiraṇyagarbha can cause this world, for they all have been created by the Lord (*Vs.*, I.4.26-27). Hence, Īshvara alone is the one single cause from whom follow origination, sustenance and retraction of this world (*Vs.*, I.4.23). Īshvara alone is both the material and efficient cause of this world (*Vs.*, I.4 23, I.4.22, 26, 27). But can we not ask the further cause of Īshvara himself? No.

> ". . . . 'on account of the impossibility', Brahman which is mere Being cannot spring from mere being, since the relation of cause and effect cannot exist without a certain superiority (i.e., not in a pure homogeneous state of Sat alone). Nor again can Brahman spring from that which is something particular, since this would be contrary to experience. For what we observe that particular forms of existence are produced from what is general, as, for instance, jars and pots from clay, but not that what is general is produced from particulars . . . . Nor does the fact of other effects springing from effects imply that Brahman (i.e., Ishvara) also must be an effect, for the non-admission of a fundamental causal substance (i.e., Ishvara) would drive us to a *regressus ad infinitum*" (*Vs.*, II.3.9).

Again, in the same para it is maintained that the world cannot spring from *asat* in the light of *Ch. U.*, VI.2.2.

> "How from non-Being could Being be produced?"

Thus, Brahman is its own ground, for existence and consciousness' (*sat* and *cit*) are identical. As a matter of fact the non-existence of Brahman cannot be even imagined. All other things, even gods and Hiraṇyagarbha, being contingent can pass away, but not Brahman itself (*BU.*, IV.2.4). This Brahma, as the creator of the world, pictured as a king is really saguṇa and not the supreme nirguṇa (*Vs.*, I.4.23).

Teleological Argument

Kant, criticising all the arguments for the existence of God, had a very soft corner for the teleological argument. According to him, it is the oldest, the clearest and the most accordant with the common reason of mankind. Hence, it has to be treated with respect.[1] For Shankara too, Brahman cannot be an object of knowledge, is beyond perception and inference. Yet he puts forth the teleological argument with a certain amount of animation.

Following very closely the view of his master, Padmapāda observes that this world cannot originate from an insentient Pradhana of Prakṛti. Even a sentient source of limited powers cannot create this which is beyond the mental conception (*Pañcapādikā*, V.4.12-13). Then more clearly Padmapāda states that this world of variegated forms is inconceivable save as the handiwork of a mighty being. As the pot cannot be thought without a potter, so the world of inconceivable forms cannot be thought without Īshvara as its creator (*Pañcapādikā*, IV.9.39). The language of Shankara himself is no less clear:

> "That omniscient and omnipotent cause from which proceed the origin, subsistence, and dissolution of this world .... which world is differentiated by names and forms, contains many agents and enjoyers, is the abode of the fruits of actions, these fruits having their definite places, times and causes, and the nature of whose arrangement cannot even be conceived by the mind .... that cause we say, is Brahman" (*Vs.*, I.1.2).

But, keeping to the evolutionary nature of the world, can we not regard the world as self-regulative, orderly and adapted by the mechanical functions of the fortuitous combinations of atoms, as was considered by the Indian atomists and later on by the Western evolutionists? Padmapāda sets aside the doctrine of self-regulative nature (*svabhāvavāda*) in the face of 'unique design' in nature. Here one has to note that Indian thinkers regarded the birth of every individual and his environment as a result of his karmas in the countless, previous births. As such for theists that unique design was of special interest. Shankara himself discounts the possibility of orderly evolution of the insentient Prakṛti. Against

[1] I. Kant, *Pure Reason*, Eng. tr. by N.K. Smith, abridged, p. 293.

the doctrine of unconscious teleology on the part of Prakṛti for the benefit of release of the spirits in bondage, Shankara states the following: (*Vs*., II.2.1).

> ". . . .We point out that a non-intelligent thing which, without being guided by an intelligent being, spontaneously produces effects capable of subserving the purposes of some particular person is nowhere observed in the world. We rather observe that houses, palaces, couches, pleasure-grounds, and the like . . . . are made by workmen endowed with intelligence."

Now, the important passage with a good deal of eloquence starts which will remind one of the arguments that David Hume puts in the mouth of theist Cleanthes:[1]

> "Now look at this entire world which appears, on the one hand, as external (i.e. inanimate) in the form of earth and the other elements enabling (the souls) to enjoy the fruits of their various actions, and, on the other hand, as animate, in the form of bodies which belong to the different classes of beings, possess a definite arrangement of organs, and are therefore capable of constituting the abodes of fruition; look, we say, at this world of which the most ingenious workmen cannot even form a conception in their minds, and then say if a non-intelligent principle like the pradhana is able to fashion it! . . . .We rather must assume that just as clay and similar substances are seen to fashion themselves into various forms, if worked upon by potters and the like, so the pradhana also is ruled by some intelligent principle" (*Vs*., II.2.1).

Here again Shankara reminds us that his reasoning is not an independent source for his theistic conclusion, but is in conformity with the teaching of the scripture. One will also note that Shankara is taking the aid of reasoning in establishing theism merely repeats the proofs already advanced by Gautama, Prashastapada and Uddyotakara. But it is doubtful whether Vācaspati Mishra and Udayana would have paid so much of their attention, if Shankara's support were not available in this regard.

[1]D. Hume, *Dialogue Concerning Natural Religion*, p. 115.

The whole doctrine of Brahman, jīva and Īshvara and māyā has the sole aim of winning one's liberation by having *jñāna* of the entities mentioned above. Therefore now we have to explain the nature and the means of obtaining liberation.

Liberation (*Mokṣa*)

Liberation simply means Brahma-realisation, and this means becoming Brahma itself. Shankara never tires of repeating this advaitic truth (*Vs.*, I.1.4) contained in (*Muṇḍ. U.*, III.2.9), 'He who knows Brahman becomes Brahman'. The reason is that a jiva is nothing but B only his nescience and the *upādhis* born of nescience have to be dissolved. Just as drops of water are dissolved in water and rivers merge into the sea (*Vs.*, I.4.21-22), so the jīva, having his limiting adjuncts dissolved, merges into Brahma. Here it is useful to picture the analogies of earthen pots and earth, the universal ākāśa limited by the enclosures of different pots and, rooms (*Vs.*, II.1.14). Every kind of manifoldness is nothing but unreal like the phantoms in a dream (*Vs.*, II.1.14), a simile which was used by Gauḍapāda himself. Nay, Shankara follows the Mādhyamikas through Gauḍapāda inasmuch as he regards both bondage and liberation as illusory, since Brahma which a jīva is and which he attains through *jñāna* is himself unproduced and unproducing:

> "But this (*mokṣa*) is eternal in the true sense, i.e., eternal without undergoing any changes (*Kuṭastha-nitya*), omnipresent as ether, free from all modifications, absolutely self-sufficient, not composed of parts, or self-luminous nature" (*Vs.*, I.1.4).

Brahma-realisation is of the following nature:

> "That Brahman whose nature it is to be at all times neither agent nor enjoyer, and which is thus opposed in being to the (soul's) previously established state of agency and enjoyment, that Brahman am I; hence I neither was an agent nor an enjoyer at any previous time, nor am I such at the present time, nor shall I be such at any future time; this is the cognition of the man who knows Brahman" (*Vs.*, IV.1.13).

This state of the absoluteness of the real Brahman-state of a jīva has been explained by a number of analogies. A jīva in a state of infatuation has been compared to a person who seeks for a garland in utter forgetfulness of the fact that garland is all the time round his neck, or else, it is just like the example of the tenth man who counting others in a party of ten men ignores counting himself all the time, and misses the tenth man every time he counts (*B.U.B.*, 1.4.7). Shankara himself recites that a child of a king being brought up by the hunters, thinks himself as belonging to the tribe of hunters. But he is a prince all the time and once he is told that he is a prince and he comes to be in this knowledge then he acquires his status which he had all the time from his birth to the moment of this realisation of his being a prince (*B.U.B.*, II.1.20). Thus, every jiva is Brahma (*BU.*, II.5.19), which realisation is nothing but *mokṣa.*

In a real sense, as Gauḍapāda and the Mahāyānists had concluded that both bondage and liberation are equally unreal. If bondage and *mokṣa* were real states of Brahman, then either they will be successive or simultaneous.

> "They cannot be simultaneous states of the Self as they are mutually opposed, just as motion and rest cannot be simultaneous states of one and the same thing. If successive, they are either caused or uncaused by another. If uncaused by another, there can be no liberation.* If caused by another, they cannot be inherent in the Self and cannot therefore by real" (*B.G.B.*, XIII.2).

As Brahman has no phases of existence (*Vs.*, IV.1.2) and, as liberation is nothing but Brahma-realisation, so the jiva is really Brahman all the time, and, as such both bondage and liberation are equally illusory:

> Brahma-realisation is a matter of *Sākṣātkāra.* "And the knowledge of Brahman which discards nescience and effects final release terminates in a perception (viz. the intuition . . . *Sākṣātkāra* . . . . of Brahman), and as such must be assumed to have a seen result . . . ." (*Vs.*, II.1.4).

Again, in *B.G.B.*, XIII.2 Shankara points out that discriminative

*But liberation is a fact as is witnessed in the case of *jīvanmukti:* "If you deny an observed fact, saying it is impossible, you would be contradicting experience, a thing which nobody will allow" (*B.U.B.*, I.4.10).

knowledge leads to a direct perception of Kṣetrajña. In like manner in *Vs.*, IV.1.1 and IV.1.2 Shankara maintains that repetition of hearing, reasoning etc. concerning the Self, may terminate in the intuition of Brahman. This kind of realisation is non-dual, different from subject-object-based reasoning (*Vs.*, I.1.4). It has been very well put by M.K.V. Iyer, *Brahma-jñāna* is intuitive, mystical and non-conceptual.[1] It is *aprokṣānubhūti* just like *aham-pratyaya.* This may be called some sort of mystic communion known as *nirvikalpaka* Samādhi.[2] This may be termed as knowledge by acquaintance, pertaining to a proper name, as Bertrand Russell calls it, or, knowledge by 'enjoyment' as distinguished, from knowledge by 'contemplation' as Samuel Alexander had put it. This mystical intuition is completely free from māyā, and wholly disengaged from matter.[3]

Karmakāṇḍa and Liberation

The *Gītā* refers to three paths of salvation, namely, *Karmayoga, Bhaktiyoga* and *Jñānayoga.* Shankara rejects the claims of *Karmakāṇḍa* and *Bhaktiyoga* in favour of *Jñānayoga.* Let us now discuss the place of *karmas* in obtaining *mokṣa* (liberation). It will not be out of place to mention the views of other Indian scholars in this connection:

1. *Karma* alone, without its intermixture with any other means, is supposed to be effective in obtaining liberation, according to Mīmāṃsā.
2. Of course, for Mīmāṃsā and for our discussion in general, by '*karma*' is meant 'Vedic rituals and sacrifice'. However, the Jainas and Bauddhas completely ignore Vedic rituals, so for them *karmas* in general mean austerities, Yogic exercises and other moral disciplines. They combine actions with knowledge, pertaining to their systems of thought.
3. *Jñāna* without work is called *Karma-Sannyāsa* and is said to be the doctrine of Sāṃkhya. In a general way this may also be said to be the stand of Nāgārjuna. This is also the predominant view of Shankara, though he concedes that *karmas* may be helpful in obtaining *jñāna* in a very secondary way.

[1]M.K.V. Iyer, *Advaita Vedanta*, p. 34.
[2]Ibid., p. 50.
[3]K.H. Potter, *EIP*, pp. 229-30.

In his doctrine of *karma* and liberation, Shankara was very much influenced by Sāṃkhya philosophy. According to Sāṃkhya, the pure spirit is pure consciousness without any activity of its own. Only Prakṛti is active (*pariṇāminitya*). Activity on the part of the embodied jīva is due to its *avidya* (infatuation) by virtue of which it participates in agency and enjoyment. Once *vivekakhyati* (discrimination-knowledge) dawns, the spirit regains its pristine state of total aloofness from all activities and realizes its former state of pure consciousness.

Now the Prakṛti of Sāṃkhya is transformed into the doctrine of nescience or māyā in the Advaitism of Shankara. Hence, *mukti* for Shankara simply means riddance from prākṛtic activities or māyika karma. Any *karma* for Shankara is a mark of bondage, and, in the same way, Brahma is pure consciousness without any activity whatsoever. Hence, liberation which is a state of Brahma-realisation, is the realization of the pristine state of pure consciousness. Naturally, for Shankara, the state of *mukti* or even *jīvanmukti* is a state of *Karma-Sannyāsa* i.e., the total renunciation of all *karmas* and duties.[1] In the same way 'knowledge' means *Brahma-jñāna* which is a state of pure consciousness (*cit*). As such a *jīvanmukta* is a renunciate who has to work if at all for maintaining his bare bodily existence (*B.G.B.*, XIV.25).

Keeping to the above-mentioned observation, for Shankara, knowing i.e., *Brahma-Sākṣātkāra* is not an act.[2] In the same way, *Brahma-jñāna* is not *upāsana* (worship). It is not even yogic sādhanā, for this is also an act. Of course, Shankara does not deny the place of worship and yogic exercises, as also of Vedic Karmas. But their place is only secondary, external and at most preparatory. They bring the seeker to the brink of the promised land of liberation. But only when the seeker is awakened into his pristine state of pure consciousness, he can have release. This awakening may be likened to 'insight' which W. Köhler noticed in his apes in reaching the solution of their problem. The insightful learning, according to Köhler, takes place with lightning-like suddenness and once it occurs, the ape never loses it. In the same manner when the seeker obtains Brahma-realisation, he never again slides back into *sāṃsārika* existence. Therefore, Shankara, favours *mukti* through

[1] *B.G.B.*, II.21; also Introduction to II.10.
[2] K.H. Potter, *EIP*, *Upadeśasahasri*, p. 244.

mahāvākyas and in general does not favour *karma-mukti* i.e., liberation through progressive stages.

For Shankara, therefore, Brahma-realisation can be achieved only through *bodhi*, enlightenment or genuine awakening. Shankara utterly disregards the role of *karma* in directly achieving liberation. His argument in this regard is most anti-*Ṛgvedic*. He even does not favour the doctrine of *Jñāna-Karma-Samuccayavāda* where *Brahma-jñāna* is combined with *karma*.[1] The reason is that Prakṛti and the spirit are opposed, so in like manner, act and knowing too are mutually exclusive.

Shankara and his followers have presented a great many arguments against the claim of *karmas* in achieving liberation. The most important arguments against *karma*-docrine is that liberation is eternal, unborn and non-originated. However, a *karma* can achieve a result which can only be temporary, for whatever is achieved or whatever has a beginning must have an end. Hence, through *karma* there can be no eternal liberation. Secondly, *karma* of its very nature implies an actor, act, instruments, the object and some motive or desire. Hence, *karma* implies differentiation. But Brahma is undifferenced. Hence, undifferentiated Brahma-realisation cannot be achieved through *karmas*.

For Shankara, all acts even *nitya-karmas* are tainted with desires,[2] and, where there is desire, there can be no liberation. Again, actions are always accompanied with egoism,[3] and, egoism means that the identity of jiva-Brahma has not been reached. Without this identity there can be no liberation.

Besides, the Mīmāṃsakas are opposed to the advaitic theory, according to which, *jñāna* and *jñāna* alone is the only way to attain *mukti*. According to the Mīmāṃsakas through action alone liberation can be achieved. They, however, teach that one should abstain from *kāmya* and *niṣiddha karmas*, but should perform *nitya* and *naimittika karmas*, for obtaining *mukti*. Even when they like Kumarila combine *jñāna* with *karmas*, they make *jñāna* subservient to rituals, sacrifice, meditation and other actions. The doctrine of *Jñāna-Karma-Samuccayavāda* was advocated by pre-Shankara advaitins

[1] *B.G.B.*, II.10; also introductory commentary.

[2] Karl H. Potter, *EIP*, p. 182; Introduction to *B.G.B.*, where *jñāna* and *karma* are stated to be utterly opposed.

[3] Ibid., pp. 229-30.

like Brahmadatta, Bhartṛprayañca and above all Maṇḍana Mishra.[1]

When Shankara controverts the position of *Karmakāṇḍa*, then he always has the views of the Mīmāmsakas and Maṇḍana Mishra in his mind. In a general way, Shankara is highly critical of Vedic *Karmakāṇḍa* which formed the main contributions of the Vedic Āryans. It is such an irony that Shankara keeping to Āryan Brahminism is so critical of the Āryan contributions to Hinduism, and, as against this upholds the non-Āryan cult of *jñāna* taught by the *Upanishads*, *Sāṃkhya*, *Vijñānavāda* and *Shūnyavāda*. However, Shankara felt the truth of *Jñānayoga* so deeply and so strongly that nothing could dislodge him from this stirring conviction.

All *karmas*, for Shankara, are essentially painful and are the products of ignorance *B.G.B.*, II.21. Hence, in a general way, Shankara has no place for Vedic works in his scheme of *Jñānayoga*. Later on, he at most, accords a secondary place to works.

First, Brahma is neither an agent nor an enjoyer, and, in the state of liberation, a jīva becomes Brahma itself. Hence, in his real nature, no agency belongs to a jiva.

> "For if being an agent belongs to the soul's nature, it can never free itself from it . . . . no more than fire can divest itself of heat, ... and as long as man has not freed himself from activity he cannot obtain his highest end, since activity is essentially painful." (*Vs.*, II.3.40).

Hence, agentship and activity are due to avidyaic adjuncts (*Vs.*, II.3.40) and as such due to nescience (*B.U.B.*, IV.4.10; *G.B.*, II.21). Further, Shankara in *B.G.B.*, XIII.2 holds that Vedic injunctions and prohibitions of the Śāstras concern only the ignorant. Commenting on *BU.*, IV.4.10 and *Muṇḍ. U.*, I.2.9, Shankara says that persons in ignorance enter into blinding darkness, but they who pride in their knowledge of *Karmakāṇḍa* enter into greater darkness. Again, commenting on *B.G.*, XV.I, Shankara very harshly passes judgement on *Karmakāṇḍa*, for according to him, it pertains to perpetuate the avidyaic existence of Samsāra. The reason for this denunciation is not far to seek. The Vedic works have the aim of obtaining desires for progeny, worldly prosperity and temporary happiness of heaven (*B.G.B.*, II.42-44; VIII.20; *Vs.*, I.1.4; III.4.12). Naturally people

J. Kattackal, *Religion and Ethics in Advaita*, pp. 152-57.

having desires cannot obtain final liberation. Hence, Shankara rejects *Karmayoga* for obtaining liberation:

> "And as nobody is able to show any other way in which Release could be connected with action, it is impossible that it should stand in any, even the slightest, relation to any action, excepting knowledge." (*Vs.*, I.1.4).

This saving knowledge has no connection whatsoever with 'Vedic statements' (*Vs.*, I.1.4), and, Shankara gives his reasons for his views.

First, Shankara keeps on quoting the *Upanishads* to show that Brahman is non-dual (*Ch. U.*, VI.2.1; *BU.*, II.5.19; *M.U.U.*, 2.11 and so on). Activity, on the other hand, logically implies duality: (*Vs.*, I.1.4).[1]

> "Every sacrificial rite, such as agnihotra, is associated with an idea of the accessories of action, such as a particular God or Gods to whom oblation should be offered, and with egoism on the part of the agent and his attachment for the result." (*B.G.B.*, IV.24).

Hence, in sacrificial acts there is dualism, egoism and attachment to desires. Besides, actions are for obtaining human ends only. (*S.B.G.*, VII.1).

Further, *Brahma-jñāna* leads to eternal liberation (*Vs.*, I.1.4) and to this aspect reference has already been made. In contrast, works can produce an effect, and, any produced effect is non-eternal. Nay, at most the result of Vedic works can lead one to heavenly happiness which is ephemeral (*Vs.*, I.1.1; I.1.4; *B.G.B.*, IX.21; *Vs.*, III.4. 32). Thirdly, the *Vedas* themselves are valid only empirically and when *Brahma-jñāna* dawns, then they too finally disappear:

> "For, the final authority teaches that the Self is in reality no percipient of objects, and while so denying, the *Veda* itself ceases to be an authority, just as the dream-perception in the waking state." (*B.G.B.*, II.69).

[1]Again, action, according to Shankara, involves the differences of action, agent and fruzt (K.H. Potter, *EIP*, *A.U.B.*, p. 273).

For this reason, the trusted disciple of Shankara, namely, Padmapāda in his *Pañcapādikā* describes the validity of the Śāstras for the people living in the realm of nescience (I.38.142, p. 107; I.41. 157, p. 117; I.38.146, pp. 109-40). Hence, Shankara completely discounts the claim of works for obtaining *B-jñāna*:

> "The special question with regard to the enquiry into Brahman is whether it presupposes as its antecedent the understanding of the acts of religious duty (which is acquired by means of the Purva Mīmāmsā). To this question we reply in the negative. . . ." (*Vs.*, I.1.1).

Nay, more. Vedic injunctions, for Shankara,

> ". . . . are ineffective because they refer to something which cannot be enjoined, just as the edge of a razor becomes blunt when it is applied to a stone." (I.1.4).

Thus, for Shankara, Vedic action does not stand in the slightest relation to knowledge (*Vs.*, IV.3.14). In this connection, this is the conclusion of Shankara:

> "And the knowledge of that Self does not only not promote action but rather cuts all action short[1]. . . . Hence the view of reverend Badarayana . . . . remains valid and cannot be shaken by fallacious reasoning about the subordination of knowledge to action and the like." (*Vs.*, III.4.8; ref. III.4.15, 17; *Vs.*, I.1.4).

Shankara regards *Karmakāṇḍa* for purposes different from those of *Jñānayoga* (*Vs.*, I.1.4; III.4.12; *B.G.B.*, II.42-48; VII.20). These two paths can be said to be lower and higher respectively.

> "Of the lower one it is said that it comprises the *Ṛgveda* and so on, and then the text continues, 'The higher knowledge is that by which the Indestructible is apprehended'." (*Vs.*, I.2.21).

And as has been mentioned, even the Vedic gods fall short of *B-jñāna* though they are qualified for it (*Vs.*, I.3.33). However, there

[1]K.H. Potter, *EIP*, *A.U.B.*, p. 271.

are a number of passages where Shankara accords a secondary value to Vedic works:

> "It is only when the rites have purified them, that people, with their minds pure, can easily know the Self that is revealed by the *Upanishads.*" (*B.U.B.*, IV.4.22).

Again, works help in washing away uncleanliness and purify the mind, and, in this way prepare the seeker for attaining knowledge of the highest (*Vs.*, III.4.27; III.4.34; IV.1.18). They may also have a long term effect in future successive rebirths of the individual. Works in this life may lead to rebirth as a human being with some favourable circumstances, in the next rebirth in a good family, and, thus gradually perfected, they may contribute indirectly for reaching the highest state of knowledge (*Vs.*, III.4.5).[1] Should we,

[1]From these and other remarks some advaitic thinkers specially the author of *Bhāmatī* has accorded an instrumental value of works. G. Jha has mentioned that according to the author of *Bhāmatī*, works produce eagerness for liberation (*Vividisa*). The steps in the *Bhāmatī* can be thus mentioned.

For preparing oneself for knowledge (*Brahma-jñāna*) *karmas* may be helpful in the same way in which self-control, calmness etc., are helpful. Of course, Shankara regards calmness etc., as of greater usefulness in this context than works (*Vs.*, III.4.27). But, according to *Bhāmatī* the whole process with regard to works as an auxiliary aid may be thus mentioned:

(a) The performance of Varṇa-āśrama dharmas produces merit.
(b) This Merit dissolves all sin and evil, for the continuance of *avidya* has its root in Demerit.
(c) When evil gets dispelled, man through his perception and reasoning realises that Sāṃsāric existence is essentially painful (cp. *Nitya-anitya vastu-viveka*).
(d) As a result of this dissatisfaction, the spirit of detachment dawns in relation to the world (cp. *Ihamutrartha-bhoga-viraga*).
(e) Then there is the eagerness to get rid of this dissatisfaction.
(f) Through the help of the scripture and teacher, he learns that *Brahma-jñāna* is the only way to liberation.
(g) Then he becomes eager to search for *Brahma-jñāna* (*Vs.*, I.1.14), where Shankara refers to the rousing of the desire for *Brahma-jñāna* or *mumukṣutva*.
(h) When he really becomes *mumukṣu*, then alone *śravaṇa*, *manana* and *nididhyāsana* become effective.

The *Bhāmatī* concludes:

'Thus, it stands to reason that rites are remote auxiliaries in respect of the generation of knowledge, through the purification of *Sattva* i.e., the intellect.' The *Bhāmatī Catussutri*, Eng. tr. by S.S. Suryanarayana Sastri and C. Kunhan Raja, p. 85.

therefore, judging from the instrumentality of works and their purifying function, advance the doctrine of *Jñāna-Karma-Samuccaya-vāda?* In his preliminary commentary on *B.G.*, II.11, Shankara discounts this possibility altogether. According to Shankara, it is erroneous and even impossible to think about the possibility of the combination of *jñāna* and *karma,* for according to him, no such *samuccaya* has ever been entertained in the *Gītā,* secondly[1] *Karma-yoga* is meant for the ignorant (*B.G.B.*, II.21), and for people of this world only (*B.G.B.*, IV.12).

Further, action presupposes ignorance, and, by contrast, *B-jñāna* presupposes abstaining from action.[2] This matter was further taken by Sureshvara who criticizes Maṇḍana's theory of *prasaṅkhyāna*, for this is, according to Sureshwara an act.

But is not *jñāna* itself an action?

No. *Jñāna* is not an action, for *karma* is dualistic but *jñāna* in Shankara's sense is not dualistic. Of course, ordinary knowledge is analysed into knowing, the object known and the content of knowing. But Shankara means by *jñāna* in which knowing means becoming Brahman itself, which state is the eternal being of the jīva. Knowing for Shankara is not an achievement-verb. Hence, knowing means Brahma-realisation which is always *sat*, without any distinction, within or without.

Connected with above-mentioned point, Shankara contrasts knowing from action. An action, according to Shankara, has four characteristics, namely:

(i) The origination (*utapatti*) of a thing viz., making of a pot.
(ii) Change of a position in space e.g., going to a city or home.
(iii) An action may lead either the purification or otherwise of one's *saṃskāra*.
(iv) An action may effect some modification e.g. melting of butter. But *jñāna* is none of these, for *jñāna* is liberation which is not going to heaven or achieving any result, but is

G. Jha has referred to the above stages, according to the *Naiṣkarmyasiddhi* by Sureshvaracarya (ibid., p. 252; Ref. *Naiṣkarmyasiddhi*, Hindi tr., chap. I, *Vs.*, 45, 47, 49, 50).

[1]cp. *B.U.B.*, IV.4.9 where god works and knowledge are said to be mutually contradictory. In this context, vide *B.U.B.*, I.4.10; III.3.1; *Naiṣkarmyasiddhi*, chap. I, verse 55.

[2]Again, action, according to Shankara, involves the differences of action, agent and fruit (K.H. Potter, *EIP*, *A.U.B.*, p. 273).

the realisation of one's eternal state of pure and undifferentiated consciousness.

Lastly, for Shankara, the *Vedas* themselves are sublated when *B-jñāna* dawns. Therefore, Vedic Karmas have to be discarded with Brahma-realisation.

Thus, Shankara is very critical of *Karmayoga* and does not favour *Karma-Jñāna-Samuccaya.* In comparison, he is favourably inclined towards theistic worship, even though he regards it as a means only for ultimately leading to *jñāna-niṣṭhā.*

Worship and Liberation

According to Shankara *upāsana* (worship) is the concentration of the mind on a symbol (*ālambana* or support) prescribed by the Śāstras. When the mind gets concentrated and there is a steady flow of the mental stream in the direction of the symbol by warding off all disturbing thoughts, then there results *sattva-śuddhi* (purification of the mind).[1] In due course, this mental purification becomes a stage for gaining *B-jñāna* which is the same thing as liberation (cp., Introduction to *Ch. U.*; *Bhāṣya* I.1.1).

Further, according to Sureshvara, meditation on a symbol is an act, and, no act can lead to liberation.[2] But certainly it is a preparatory aid for obtaining *B-jñāna.* Of course, worship always involves dualism and Brahma is non-dual. Hence, there can be no B-realisation through worship.

Īshvara is only a māyic Being and is ultimately limited by *upādhis* (adjuncts) born of nescience (*Vs.*, III.2.11-12). As such He is an object of worship for people as yet under the spell of māyā. Hence, liberation proper cannot be due to worship (which is possible for people in *avidya*), nor can the attainment of Īshvara be final, for He is not non-dual but has a number of powers (*Vs.*, III.3.23). Shankara whilst commenting on *B.G.*, III.36 mentions six attributes of 'Bhagavāna or Īshvara', namely, perfect dominion, might, glory, splendour, dispassion and salvation. All these six attributes have been admitted by *Viṣṇu Purāṇa*, *Āḷvārs* and *Pāñcarātra.* Besides, Īshvara not being non-dual does not pertain to B-realisation of non-dual existence, for in worship the dualism of the worshipper and worshipful can never be overcome. Again, the worshippers

[1]K.H. Potter, *EIP*, *Ch. U.B.*, p. 255.
[2]Ibid., pp. 242, 255, 428, 430, 600.

having various *saṃskāras* and tendencies worship for obtaining various ends and pray to different gods.

> "For devout meditations on the qualified Brahman may, like acts, be either identical or different. Scripture moreover teaches that, like acts, they have various results; some of them have visible results, others unseen results, and others again—as conducive to the springing up of perfect knowledge- have for their result by successive steps." (*Vs.*, III.3.1; also ref. *Vs.*, I.1.11; I.1.24; III.2.21).

The people worship the Lord for gaining Lordship (*Vs.*, IV.3.14), gradual liberation (*Vs.*, III.2.21), some others for earthly prosperity and perhaps for happiness in the next life (*Vs.*, IV.12), and still others for warding off calamities (*Vs.*, III.2.21). Shankara, quoting the *Gītā* states 'In whatever form they meditate on him, that they become.' (*Vs.*, I.1.11; IV.1.15).

> "I reward men by granting them the things they desire, just in accordance with the way in which they seek Me and the motive with which they seek Me; for they donot seek for *mokṣa*" IV.II. (*B.G.*, IV.11; see *B.S.G.*, VII; 16-25).

The difference in having various motives, rites and gods depends on the *saṃskāras* of the previous births.

> "Those whose wisdom has been led astray by this or that desire resort to other gods, engaged in this or that rite, constrained by their own nature." (*B.G.*, VII.20).

However, for gaining their objective, each worshipper has to worship with full devotion and faith (*B.G.*, VII.21-22; IX.23, 26).

> "Votaries of the gods go to gods; to the Pitris (ancestors) go to the votaries of the pitris; to the Bhutas (spirits) go the worshippers of the spirits; My worshippers come to Myself." (*B.G.*, IX.25; also vide *Vs.*, I.1.24).

Even though worship is tainted by duality, desires and of various lower gods, yet it has not to be set aside (*Vs.*, III.2.21), because it may mean a means to the highest Brahman (III.3.14).

First, they who seek lordship over the worlds do get it through meditation, even though this fruit falls within the sphere of Saṃsāra and nescience. This lordship means immense powers and the worshipper becomes as powerful as the Lord, except His creatorship which belongs to the Lord alone (*Vs.*, IV.4.17). Nay, more, such worshippers having gained lordship donot return to the world.

> "And as those also who rely on the knowledge of the qualified Brahman in the end have recourse to that (Nirvana), it follows that they also do not return."
>
> (*Vs.*, IV.4.22; also see IV.2.9).

How?

They do not immediately gain the highest, but do so successively at the time of *pralaya* (i.e., periodic dissolution of the world).

> "When the reabsorption of the effected Brahman world draws near, the souls in which meanwhile perfect knowledge has sprung up proceed, together with Hiraṇyagarbha the ruler of that world, to 'what is higher than that', i.e., to the pure highest place of Viṣṇu. This is the release by successive steps which we have to accept on the basis of the scriptural declarations about the non-return of the souls." (*Vs.*, IV.3.10).[1]

Here, we can conclude with the popular recitation mentioned by G. Jha:[2]

> "Mergence into Brahma is the highest stage; lower than that is the stage of hymn-singing and repeating Mantras, and external worship is the lowermost stage."

Here we can also give the beautiful observation of Appaya Dikṣita

> "O Lord, I have in my weakness, committed three sins and I

[1]Maṇḍana maintains that this non-returning is only relative, for without *B-jñāna* the *bhakta* will have to return at the next cyclic creation (K.M. Potter, ibid., *Brahmasiddhi*, p. 406).

[2]G. Jha, *Shānkara Vedanta*, p. 255.

beg forgiveness of you. To serve as a support for meditation I have given a form to the Highest who is really formless; I have tried to define the indefinable by composing stotras and litanies and lastly I have confined the omnipresent Lord to particular places of worship and have journeyed to those places."[1]

Critical Comments with Regard to Shankara's Theism

Now we are in a position to discuss the remarks of Deussen and Dasgupta who regard the concept of Īshvara as only secondary and of no importance.[2] In the light of the system and actual statements of Shankara, the place of theism in Shankara Advaitism cannot be regarded either as purely secondary or of 'little importance'. Meditation of Īshvara is not secondary, for the relationship between Īshvara and Brahman is of very close proximity (*Vs.*, IV.3.9) and as such worship can lead to *Brahma-jñāna.* Besides, we have already seen that meditation directly leads to the stage of successive liberation ending in the realisation of the highest (*Vs.*, IV.3.10; IV.4.22).

We also do not think that Īshvara, being māyika and phenomenal is of little importance in the system of the *Vedānta.* Without accepting the status and function of Īshvara, the whole phenomenal world becomes inexplicable Creation of the World at the beginning of a new Kalpa will remain inexplicable. Besides, Shankara does not say so, but the statements of the *Gītā* to which Shankara pays sufficient attention suggests that the people belonging to different typology and function (as C.G. Jung would say) on account of their past *saṃskāras* cannot help worshipping Īshvara. Hence, men cannot live without Īshvara. This is what is known as *religion a priori.* This is the point involved in the worship of Īshvara by *consensus gentium* to which Udayana refers in his *Kusumāñjali.*

If Shankara were not a committed theist, then he would not have composed a number of beautiful hymns. As a matter of fact he was a great theistic devotee. His hymns in *Stotra-Ratānvalī* and the most lyrical hymn *Bhaja Govindam*[3] will easily place him among the great *bhaktas* of the world. As a matter of fact he has

[1]M.K.V. Iyer, *Advaita Vedanta,* p. 200.

[2]S.N. Dasgupta, *A History of Indian Philosophy,* vol. I, p. 477; Paul Deussen, *The System of the Vedanta,* p. 279.

[3]T.M.P. Mahadevan, *The Hymns of Śaṅkara.*

been called an inseparable blending of Ramakrishna of Swami Vivekananda. Because, Shankara was a theist, so he had undertaken to reform the organisations of many temples. Besides, in the four maṭhas, theistic worship is even now in vogue. Not only this, but he permitted the worship of any God or gods, according to the *saṃskāras* of the worshippers, exactly as the *Gītā* has laid down (*B.G.*, IX.30). The catholocity and relativity of gods and worship not only paves the way for the mutual dialogue between the warring camps of different religions, but also prepares the ground for the world unity of religions. Further, for Shankara, theistic worship is not only a very valuable aid for *mumukṣu*, but also leads to *karma-mukti* 'salvation by successive steps' (*Vs.*, IV.3.10). For all practical purposes, however, as long as this phenomenal world lasts, Īshvara will remain the most real object of worship (*Vs.*, II. 1.14). By mere, talking of the transcendental state of affairs, none should try to forget their duties and realities of the phenomenal world which still remains too much with us. Only when Brahma-realisation dawns then alone theism is given up. But this realisation is as rare as it is the most precious thing of human search.

Again, Shankara has accepted all the proofs for the existence of Īshvara which reason demands. And but for Shankara, Maṇḍana Mishra and probably Udayanācārya would not have given themselves to theistic proofs.

Again, Shankara does not object to the worship of Vasudeva and also of Saṃkarṣaṇa, Pradyumna and Aniruddha. He also admits that by the temple-worship of Vasudeva by means of offerings, prayers and meditation, one reaches Vasudeva Himself, who is pure knowledge and the highest reality.

> "Nor do we wish to contend against the devotional approach and the unceasing one-pointed meditation on God; for this has been recommended both by Shruti and Smṛti"[1] (*Vs.*, II.2. 42).

But Shankara does not agree with the Bhāgavatas or Vaiṣṇavas in regarding the individual souls to have been created and that they are destructible.

[1]Vide *BU.*, IV.4.23; *B.G.*, XI.55.

Thus, we conclude that Shankara in practice and theory permitted and practised theistic worship. As such in Shankara's Advaitism, theism is neither secondary nor unimportant, even though Īshvara cannot be accorded the status of the highest ontological reality of Brahman, the only non-dual reality without a second.

Lost but not the least, theistic worship is a powerful means for attaining *Brahma-jñāna*. Hence, knowing full well the short comings of theism according to his strictly monistic system Shankara points out that the worship is not to be set aside. (*Vs*., III.2.21).

According to Shankara, wtthout admitting Īshvara, the phenomenal reality of the empirical world, with fixed and designed order cannot be explained. Again, no worship is possible without its proper object called 'Īshvara' and this worship is a possible means of attaining *B-jñāna* at least indirectly and is also a means of having *krama-mukti*. However, Shankara did not encourage theistic worship, for it may lead to goals other than *B-jñāna*. Theistic worship may also be conducted for having lordship (*Vs*., IV.3.14), or *svarga-prapti* (*Vs*., IV.1.2), or for *krama-mukti*. Again, theistic worship may be used tamasically for gaining worldly prosperity. But those who seek Brahman should worship Īshvara with a view to reaching the goal of differenceless Brahman, successively and gradually, as is implied in the meditation on *Om*.

In relation to Shankara's philosophy of a world religion a number of senior teachers of philosophy have raised the objection, 'Has not Shankara instead of explaining religion (rather theism) really explained it away?' Here one has to note the distinction between religious philosophy and religion in practice. Religious language of philosophy is *about* religion and is not itself a religion. In the language of Shankara the Vedāntic philosophy must commit a happy suicide after Brahma-realisation. Hence Shankara's religious philosophy does explain theism as far as it is possible to do so in the service of Brahma-realisation.

Stages of Worship

Shankara has not clearly given us the stages of worship in terms of the hierarchical objects of meditation. However, he does mention that there can be 'successively progressing cognition' terminating into the intuition of Brahman. Why is it so? For the impartite and undifferentiated Brahman comes to be illusorily viewed with the body, the senses, the manas, the *buddhi*, the objects of the senses, and so on.

> "Now by one act of attention (i.e., by one repetition of *shravaṇa, manana* etc.) we may discard one of there parts, and by another act of attention another part; so that a successively progressing cognition may very well take place." (*Vs.*, IV.1.3).

Of course, the passage quoted above does not mention the actual stages which were mentioned by Gauḍapāda. According to Gauḍapāda, one has to meditate on *Om* which consists of a *a*, *u*, *m*, and the last *amatra* or *ardhamatra*. Each letter corresponds to three objects of worship in a hierarchical order. The letter *a* represents *Viśva* i.e., gross body composed of all the compounded elements. It stands the lowest and has been likened to the waking state. We worship such a god for obtaining worldly desires. The next stage corresponds to *u* where the deity is pictured with subtle elements and is called *Taijasa*. It is likened to a state of dreaming. Worship of such a deity, according to Guaḍapāda increases knowledge and contributes to the evenness of mind. There is a still higher stage of *Prājña* which corresponds to the letter *m* of *Om*. This has been likened to the state of dreamless sleeping. By worshipping a deity in the stage of *Prājña*, one enters the path of gods. However, only by the worship of a deity without any quality and differentiation, one gets release. This state has been likened to the *turiya* state of samādhi. Naturally this means that meditation can lead to the intuition of Brahman.

Shankara has not repeated these stages of worship in an ascending order. But he has stated that meditation on *Om* is the best help and the highest (*B.U.B.*, V.1.1).

> "Just as the image of Viṣṇu or any other god is regarded identical with that god (for purposes of worship), so is *Om* to be treated as Brahman." (*B.U.B.*, V.1.1).

Through his *Om*, according to Shankara, one knows whatever is to be known. Hence, it is the best means of Self-realisation (*B.U.B.*, V.1.1). Naturally by subscribing to the importance of *Om*, indirectly he also accepted the various stages of worship. *Om* is said to be both higher and lower Brahman (*B.G.B.*, VIII.11) and quoting (*Praśna Up.*, V.5) holds that through meditation on the three lettered, *Om* one enters the region of Brahman.

Why should one worship Brahman through *Om*? The reason is that Brahman by itself is too difficult to be meditated upon without adequate preparation. But the highest Brahman can be meditated upon through its symbols of Āditya etc. Here a contemplation on Brahman is superimposed on its symbols, analogously as the contemplation on Viṣṇu is superimposed on his images (*Vs.*, IV.1.5). What is the principle of suprimposition here?

> ". . . . the idea of something higher is to be suprimposed upon something lower, as when we view . . . . and speak of . . . . the king's charioteer as a king . . . . to act contrary to it would be disadvantageous; for should we view a king as a charioteer, we should thereby lower him, and that would not be beneficial" (*Vs.*, IV.1.5).

Hence a symbol of Brahman should point to Brahman but must not be treated as Brahman, for a symbol is qualitied. However, Brahman is without any attributes whatsoever. Hence a symbol has to be meditated upon only as a representation of Brahman, just as the image of Viṣṇu is a symbol of Viṣṇu.

Finaly, every form of the worship of the symbols of Brahman has to be left behind as we find in the teaching of Gauḍapāda's meditation of *Om*.

Liberation through Jñāna

The point to note is that, according to Shankara, jīva and Brahman are identical. *Upādhis* born of nescience obstruct the vision of this identity. This identity therefore can be established either by successively removing the *upādhis* by repeating the instructions given by a *jīvanmukta* guru (*Vs.*, IV.1.2), or, by having direct intuition of Brahman (*Vs.*, 1.3.13, pp. 172, 172n) through a new knowledge by means of *mahāvākyas*. And in any case this liberation, that is, the realisation of the identity of the jīva and Brahma can be achieved only through knowledge:

> "In the *Upanishads* nothing is spoken of as a means to the attainment of the highest end of man except the knowledge of the identity of the self and Brahman."

Again:

> ". . . . really we know of no other means of liberation except the knowledge of Brahman" (*B.U.B.*,1.4.7).

Brahma-jñāna is not mere intellectual cognition. It is spiritual illumination. Hence, the seeker at first has to undergo preparatory exercise in order that he may become fit (an *adhikārī*) for having *B-jñāna.* It means that the seeker should acquaint himself with such esoteric saying of the *Upanishads* as Tajjalān (*taj ja lān*) which according to Shankara means 'coming, ceasing, breathing.'[1] However, T.M.P. Mahadevan has further amplified the interpretation of this secret mantra. According to him it means 'that which generates (*ja*) the universe, reabsorbs (*li*) it, and sustains it.[2] In the same way, the seeker has to learn the secret significance of *Om*, to which reference has already been made. However, Shankara has made reference to the following steps to be followed by a seeker in order that he may become qualified for attaining *Brahma-jñāna* (*B.U.B.*, 1.4.7; also *Śrībhāṣya*, pp. 10-11).

1. *Nityānitya-vastuviveka* i.e., the seeker should learn to discriminate between things as eternal and non-eternal, with a view to withdrawing himself from all that is non-eternal.
2. *Iha-mutrārtha-bhogha-virāga* i.e., the seeker has to develop an attitude of complete indifference to the enjoyments of this or the other world.
3. *Shama-Dama-Sādhanā-Sampat* i.e., together it means the cultivation of quiescence (*shama*), self-restraint (*dama*), abstinence (*uparati*), endurance (*titikṣā*), contemplative concentration (*samadhana*) and faith (*śraddhā*). Faith means belief in the spiritual teacher and teachings of the *Vedānta*.
4. *Mumukṣutva* i.e., longing for release.* After this, the seeker becoming qualified for attaining *B-jñāna* has to repair to a qualified i.e., a *jīvanmukta* guru for receiving further instructions. (*Muṇḍ U.B.*, 1.2.12-13). The necessity of finding out a proper preceptor is insisted upon by Shankara. Nay, this point is so valued that for proving the existence of Īshvara, it

[1]Paul Deussen, *The System of the Vedanta*, p. 50.
[2]T.M.P. Mahadevan, *Gauḍapada*, p. 232.
*For some more detail, see K.H. Potter, *EIP*, *Ātmanātmaviveka*, p. 329.

is pointed out that without Īshvara as a teacher it would not be possible for man either to have the knowledge of craft or language. Hence, at the beginning of a new creation, Īshvara as a teacher is considered a necessity.

The teacher finding out the seeker as an *adhikārī* (qualified) instructs him in the *Upanishads* and their esoteric teaching. This is the stage of *śravaṇa* (hearing or listening with a receptive mind). Then the seeker has to reason about the truth which has been conveyed to him by the teacher. This state of ratiocination is known as *manana*. Lastly, after the seeker has heard the truth and becomes convinced of it, he has to realise *B-jñāna* by constant meditation, as has been taught in the Yoga. This is known as *nididhyāsana*.

There are eight *Shanti Vākyas* (aphorisms) which have been specially chosen by Shankara to emphasize non-difference between the jīvas and Brahman, and, we know that the realisation of this non-difference leads to liberation. They are:

1. *Ekamevādvityam Brahma* (*Ch. U.*, VI.2.1). Brahma alone is the sole reality without a second.
2. *Neha nānāsti Kiñcana* (*Kaṭh. U.*, IV.11). There is no multiplicity here at all.
   Mṛtyoḥ sa mṛtyum gacchati, ya iha nāneva pashyati (*Kaṭh. U.*, IV.11). He goes from death to death who seems to see a difference here.
3. *Tad Yo/ham so/sau, Yo/sau so/ham* (*Īśā.*, 16). He who is yonder, yonder (Purusha or B) that I am.
4. *Etadatmyaidam Sarvam tat tvam asi Śvetaketu* (*Ch. U.*, VI.16.3). This whole world has that (truth) as its soul. That art Thou, Śvetaketu.
5. *Aham Brahmāsmi* (*BU.*, I.4.10). I am Brahma.
6. *Ekam Sadvipraḥ bahudhā Vadanti* (*R.V.*, I.164.46). There is one Truth which the learned speak as many.
7. *Yathodakam durge Vṛṣṭam . . . . anuvidhāvati* (*Kaṭh. U.*, II.1.14-15). Just as rain-water fallen on rough ground runs hither-thither, so he who sees differences goes downwards (in different births).
8. *Brahma Veda brahmaiva bhavati* (*Muṇḍ. U.*, III.2.9). The knower of Brahma, becomes Brahma-himself.

However, the following four have been called *mahāvākyas* and are supposed to be most efficacious in achieving *B-jñāna*.

1. *Aham Brahmāsmi* (*BU.*, I.4.10).
2. *Tat Tvam Asi* (*Ch. U.*, VI.8.7). That art thou.
3. *Ayamātma Brahma* (*BU.*, II.5.19). This ātmā (Soul in the jīva) is Brahma.
4. *Prajñānam Brahma* (*Ait. U.*, III.5.3). Brahma is intelligence.

Tat Tvam Asi is called *upadeśa vākya* and is the most discussed *mahāvākya*. *Aham Brahmāsmi* is called *anusandhāna vākya* i.e. One has to repeat meditation on it with a view to realising its truth. The other two *mahāvākyas* are called *anubhava vākyas* i.e., they confirm the Truth of the *Vedānta* by way of realisation.[1]

Mithyātva (*falsity*) *of Vedānta-Vākyas and Release*

When *B-jñāna* dawns then all kinds of empirical knowledge disappear in the same way in which dream-world disappear as soon as waking takes place. This means that all scriptural, Vedic and even Vedāntic statements turn out to be illusory or *mithya*. The question arises. How can false advaitic knowledge lead to true *Brahma-jñāna?* To explicate this paradox of advaitic statements, various expedients, both Indian and western, can be used. First, this paradox of advaitic statements is just like 'the liar's paradox' with which Bertrand Russell was faced. Competent logicians do not consider now that Russell's *Theory of Description* is quite satisfactory. However, we can make use of it to elucidate this paradox.

According to Russell, there are levels of language. The language concerning a certain set of facts can be said to describe the set in a valid way. This may be called level (I). However, one may talk about this language level (I), in the same way in which (I) describes its set of facts. This use of language is also valid, but this is level no. II. But neither level I nor II can reflexively apply to itself. Following this observation of Russell, the Vedāntic learning and language may be really level no. II which refer to level no. I directly concerned with *B-jñāna*. The Vedāntic speech talks about *B-jñāna*, but is not descriptive of it. This point is further intelligible according to another classification of knowledge into knowledge

[1]K.S. Murty, *Revelation and Reason in Advaita Vedanta*.

by *acquaintance* and knowledge by description. In the light of this distinction, *Vedānta-vākyas* are description, and, in comparison with it, *B-jñāna* is knowledge by *acquaintance*. Hence, Brahma becomes a real proper name to which no description will properly apply. It is always *neti, neti*. It is just like the taste of sugar in the mouth of a dumb man. The dumb man enjoys the taste of sugar, but cannot talk about it. Similarly, the truth of Vedāntic statements is seen or verified in the higher language of *B-jñāna*. As long as *B-jñāna* does not dawn, the full significance of Vedāntic statement is not fully realised. What is true for a guru is not true at the level of pupil still at the stage of learning. Hence, the relativity and falsity of Vedāntic statements disappear in the non-empirical, non-descriptive consciousness at the level of *B-jñāna*, and, they are not false at the lower level of a seeker or learner. Let us take another expedient.

L. Wittgenstein has made use of the Platonic theory of reminiscence. Things of daily life simply serve to revive our memories about *Ideas* underlying the things. But no language can adequately describe the Idea. The use of language here is to give us a vision of the eternal ideas.[1]

In the same strain Shankara holds that the vowel 'A' is eternal, and, in comparison with this eternal 'A', the spoken or written A is false. Yet the written or spoken *a*, evokes in us the eternal A. Hence repeating in the language of Wittgenstein, we can say,

> "There are, indeed, things that cannot be put into words. They *make themselves manifest*." (*Tractatus*, 6.522).

Should we not say that Brahman cannot be talked about? It shows itself in Vedāntic statements?

We can say that Vedāntic statements lead to the vision or intuition of Brahma, where every talk is hushed and silenced. Nay, Brahma cannot be talked about. The Vedāntic statements serve to show or exhibit Brahma. These Vedāntic statements simply serve to evoke an intuition of Brahma. At this stage, the Vedāntic thinkers have used various analogies to illustrate their point of view. Some have used the analogies of crutches used by a lame man, others

[1]George Pitcher, *The Philosophy of Wittgenstein*, pp. 322-25.

have used the simile of a staircase for taking one to a certain destination. After the lame man has reached his destination, he lays aside his crutches. They are not to be used again, for after reaching Brahma, there is no return to the empirical world. Exactly in the same manner, Wittgenstein has observed about the use of his own philosophy.

> "My propositions serve as elucidations in the following way: anyone who understands me eventually recognizes them as nonsensical, when he has used them—as steps—to climb up beyond them. (He must so to speak, throw away the ladder after he has climbed up it)." (*Tractatus*, 6.54).

What Wittgenstein calls 'nonsensical' is called *Mithyātva* or false in the *Vedānta*.

In the same strain, Samuel Alexander has made a distinction between *contemplation* and *enjoyment*. He has also used the simile of rungs in a hierarchical order of Body-Mind-Deity. The lower cannot know the higher, but the higher knows (or contemplates) the lower, but cannot know itself. Mind, therefore, can know the material world, but cannot know the deity. What about itself? Mind can only *enjoy* itself, but cannot know or talk about it. In the same way we can know the Vedāntic statements, but after reaching *B-jñāna* we can only enjoy Brahma and cannot talk about it.

We can say that Vedāntic statements are not descriptive, but evocative or in the language of Ian Ramsey, they lead to discernment, or, what he calls as '*penny dropping*'. Some tilt, some shift of the puzzle-pictures may lead to a sudden illumination of the right objective of one's search. So the Vedāntic statements serve only as tilts and shifts to click a new illumination. Shankara too speaks of 'a new special kind of consciousness regarding the Self' as a result of Vedāntic statements.

> "Others say that meditation generates a new special kind of consciousness regarding the Self, through which the latter is known, and which alone removes ignorance, and not the knowledge due to the Vedic dicta about the Self." (*B.U.B.*, 1.4.7).

Even when Vedāntic statements may be false, yet they may help the seeker to realise the true *B-jñāna.* According to Sureshvara, a nightmare concerning a thief is certainly false, yet it may shock the dreamer into waking up, resulting in true knowledge of the actual state of affairs.

According to the *Bhāmatī*, the intuition of non-duality results from the formation of a particular psychosis as a result of the changes in the internal organ. As such this is not absolutely real. In other words, cognition which destroys nescience is as illusory as nescience. But the final *mithyajñāna* which eliminates *avidya,* in the long run eliminates itself. This has been compared to the fire which results from the friction of bamboos; it destroys the whole forest of bamboos, and, then in the end dies out itself.[1] Rāmānuja does not accept this explanation:

> "In the case of forest fire etc., what disappears continues to exist in states other than the previous one and this continuance in and through a chain of states obtains necessarily." (*Ved. Sang. pada*, 58).

One can easily see that Rāmānuja takes the metaphor too literally. However, the advaitic stand has been better explained in the following.

Sri Debi Prasad Chattopadhyaya in his excellent book *What is Living and What is Dead in Indian Philosophy?* pp. 307-8 takes up this point from *The Navanalanda Mahavihara Research Publication*, vol. I, pp. 18-21, by Satkari Mookherjee. The *tathagata* created a phantom woman to cure an infatuated man of his sex desire. The infatuated man becomes snared by the phantom woman. Then, the *tathagata* creates a phantom saint to instruct the infatuated man about the truth of the phantom woman. Thereby the infatuated man gets disillusioned about the phantom woman. The empirical world is just a make believe, and, *mahāvākyas* are as much illusory. But they have both intellectual, moral and spiritual value, from a pragmatic stand-point. Thus, the *mahāvākyas* have provisional or relative validity for instructing an ignorant man only.

Mahāvākyas are really *tatastha* statements. Being superficially descriptive of B, they tell us about the accidental nature of B. But they aim at taking us to the *Svarūpa* (real essential nature) of

[1]*The Bhāmatī*, note 297.

Brahman. In terms of Bradleyan distinction of 'what' (or content) and 'that' in a statement, we can say that the *What*, the content or the descriptive element is false, but the *that-aspect* is true. This point is taken up again in a slightly different context of *mahāvākyas*.

Mahāvākyas and Brahma-jñāna

As noted earlier, Shankara teaches the identity of jīva and Brahma. However, this identity is obstructed by nescience influencing *antaḥkaraṇa* by virtue of which B, is concealed; and, EW, manifoldness etc., are superimposed on Brahma. Hence, efforts are necessary either to remove the *upādhis* step by step, leading to purification of mind or *antaḥkaraṇa*, or, to directly have *B-jñāna* by attaining which *upādhis* will disappear altogether. *Mahāvākyas* have both the functions. As *upadeśa vākyas* (pertaining to instructions), they serve to remove the *upādhis*, step by step. However, they delineate the nature of Brahma too. Once the seeker grasps the full meaning by having the illumination of B, the *upādhis* naturally disappear altogether and immediately. This is specially true about the *mahāvākya Tat Tvam Asi*, which has become an object of very special attention and discussion in the post-Shankara *Vedānta*.

We can point to a thirsty man, 'Yonder is a cool stream of water.' The thirsty man goes there and gets his thirst quenched. 'Yonder is a cool stream of water' is at once an injunction and also a delineation of the truth. In the same way *Tat Tvam Asi* is both an evocative step to realise Brahma, and, also at the same time a delineation of the Self. When we talk about the illumination aspect of *Tat Tvam* and the attainment of Brahma, then once the seeker gets it, he requires no further injunction, no further repetition. Under this aspect the contention of Shankara is that hearing of *Tat Tvam Asi* does not require any injunction or repetition.

> "That is say, sentences such as, 'Thou art That,' which only delineate the nature of the Self, immediately leading to its realisation, there is no further action to be done with regard to the injunction about the realisation . . . . : for the knowledge of the Self is already attained by hearing the dictum about it. So what is the good of doing it over again."[1]

[1]*B.U.B.*, I.47, Eng. tr. Madhavananda, pp. 130-31.

However, quite an opposed teaching is given in *Vs.*, IV.1.2, where Shankara favours repetition. Here he points out that Brahma is without parts and without any distinction,

> "Yet men wrongly superimpose upon it the attribute of being made up of many parts, such as the body, the senses, the manas, the buddhi, the objects of the senses, the sensations, and so on. Now by the act of attention we may discard one of these parts, and by another act of attention another part; so that a successively progressing cognition may very well take place." (*Vs.*, IV.1.2, p. 336).

And then he concludes:

> "All this establishes the conclusion that, also in the case of cognitions of the highest Brahman the instruction leading to such cognition (rather intuition) may be repeated." (*Vs.*, IV.1.2; ibid., p. 337).

Thus, when *Tat Tvam Asi* serves as the occasion or injunction with a view to evoking illumination, then this requires repetition. However, when it delineates or embodies illumination itself of the Self, then it does not require any repetition. When *Tat Tvam Asi* assists in having intuition, then meditation and concentration (*prasaṅkhyāna*) may also be used as further aids.*

> "For hearing and so on when repeated terminate in intuition, and thus subserve a seen purpose, just as the action of beating, &c., terminates in freeing the rice grains from their husks." (*Vs.*, IV.1.1).

Maṇḍana dwells on the efficaciousness of *upāsana* and meditation for removing obstacles due to past *karmas* in attaining illumination. According to him and Vācaspati, verbal knowledge is characterized by mediacy, but release can be obtained by immediate intuition of Brahman. Hence, they recommend deep meditation (*prasaṅkhyāna*)

**Prasaṅkhyāna* may be a help as it may destory past *karmas*. See K.H. Potter, ibid., pp. 228, 444-46.

for transmuting mediate knowledge into the immediate intuition of Brahman. On the other hand, according to Sureshvara, concentration (*prasaṅkhyāna*) or *upāsana* cannot cause or produce illumination, for any produced effect can only be temporary,[1] since it is an accepted postulate of the advaitins that 'whatever is produced, effected or caused is temporary'. *B-jñāna* is unproduced and eternal, and, as such cannot be effected or produced by *prasaṅkhyāna*. According to Sureshvara, *mahāvākyas* themselves have a certain efficacy by virtue of which they mysteriously awaken the aspirant into the intuitive grasp of Brahma as is illustrated in 'Thou art the tenth man' (*daśmosi*).[2] Awakening through the hearing of the *mahāvākyas* has been compared to the waking up of the sleeping man as soon as his named is uttered. However, Sureshvara admits that *prasaṅkhyāna* has the value of preparatory discipline in aiding *bodhi* or enlightenment. Similarly, Padmapāda holds that the *mahāvākyas* generate a *vṛtti* i.e., mental psychosis in a hearer who has been previously prepared and attuned for attaining *B-jñāna*. According to Sureshvara, the following are the steps which ultimately aim at *B-jñāna*: Performance of *nitya-naimittika-karma* and rituals produce *dharmas* (merits). Dharmas lead to the destruction of sins, consequently mental purification. This leads to dissatisfaction with the world causing detachment (*vairāgya*) and also a desire thereby for liberation. This gives rise to search for the way and means and yoga-practice which leads finally to a state of no-mind (as Gauḍapāda would put it). Then the true understanding and illumination of *B-jñāna* by hearing *mahāvākyas* like *Tat Tvam Asi* etc., dawns.[3]

Apart from the doctrine of *prasaṅkhyāna*, some think that *antaḥkaraṇa* (internal organ producing ego-sense) itself has to be purified since it alone causes (*upādhis*).

The two opposed views of Shankara are difficult to reconcile. However, it can be stated that repetition and meditation serve to remove the obstacle standing in the way of obtaining *B-jñāna*. As soon as the obstacles have been removed, the *mahāvākyas* like *Tat Tvam Asi*, directly lead to the immediate intuition of Brahman.[4] In other words, if adequate preparatory processes have already been

[1] *Naiṣkarmyasiddhi*, verse 117.

[2] *N.S.*, III.9; III.105-6; Jacob Kattackal, *Religion and Ethics in Advaita*, p. 170.

[3] Jacob Kattackal, *Religion and Ethics in Advaita*, p. 161.

[4] T.M.P. Mahadevan, *The Philosophy of Advaita*, pp. 271-74.

completed, then immediate release follows.[1]

Jīvanmukti

In the state of emancipation, man gets freed from all evil. 'As a snake is freed from its skin, so is he freed from evil' (*Vs.*, 1. 3.13. No doubt, a released soul goes beyond good and evil. Such a person is called a *jīvanmukta* (i.e., a soul released in this earthly existence). This corresponds to the Buddhist doctrine of an Arhat. Does a *jīvanmukta* leave the body immediately? No. For the body is the result of action. Knowledge destroys all the past accumulated *karma* called (*Sañcita*) and cancels the results of current action (*Kriyamāna*). But fructescent (*prārabdha karmas*) will continue to work till they are exhausted:

> ". . . . since the resultant of the present body must produce definite results, speech, mind and the body are bound to work even after the highest realisation, for actions that have begun to bear fruit are stronger than knowledge; as, for instance, an arrow that has been let fly continues its course for some time." (*B.U.B.*, I.4.7; also vide I.4.10, p. 168).

But it will be wrong to suppose that *jīvanmukta* can perform evil or immoral action. Here is a misjudgment of A. Jacob:

> "The line of argument adopted by the commentator, and also by other apologists, is unsafe, and does not get rid of the fact that some of the upanishads, the chief source of the *Vedānta* doctrine, do without any qualification, declare that sin and virtue are alike to one knows Brahma; and the system is therefore rightly charged with immorality."

Of course, all past immoral acts are burnt up by knowledge. They disappear altogether. But can a *jīvanmukta* still having a body with *B-jñāna* do evil? No. Why? Because:

> ". . . . wrong perceptions donot arise in a man of realisation, for there is then no object for them."[2]

[1]K.H. Potter, *EIP*, *Upadeśasahasri*, pp. 246-57; *Naiṣkarmyasiddhi*, pp. 537-38.
[2]*B.U.B.*, I.4.19; K.H. Potter, *EIP*, vol. III, p. 257.

But unlike a Bodhsattva, a *jīvanmukta* cannot serve humanity. He can at best be a preceptor to qualified pupils. Final release comes only with the fall of the body, when even *prārabdha karmas* get exhausted. (*B.U.B.*, I.4.10; p. 169).

Yet a *jīvanmukta* has to engage himself in the barest bodily activities for maintaining his life.[1]

It is the awareness which alone makes a difference. A true renunciate . . . . rises above every distinction, and every emotion. Only an authentic seeker finds in the *jīvanmukta* the flood gate of eternity in the temporal flow of his bare existence. He enjoys complete equanimity of mind. No, he has attained the state of no mind as Gauḍapāda has put it. As such loses the capacity of pleasure pain, hunger-thirst, anger-hatred. Neither action nor *upāsana* nor renunciation has any meaning for him. As stated above he becomes *Kuṭastha nitya.*

For Shankara, the state of *jīvanmukti* is an experienced event in the life of a seeker for *Brahma-jñāna*. Might be, this experience may be due to intensive endoctrination as contained in *śravaṇa-manana,* or, else this experience of *jīvanmukta* may be the effect of the Yogic exercise in emptying out all thoughts, reaching a state of pure blank called *turiya,* or, it may be due to auto-suggestion in the state of *nididhyāsana*. However, with a view to silencing all objections, Shankara asks:

> 'How can one's own intimate experience of Brahma knowledge, while still embodied, can be contested by any body else?' (*Vs.*, IV.1.15).

The reality of *jīvanmukti* can also be supported by the various *Upanishads*, e.g., *BU.*, IV.4.7 holds that *Brahma-jñāna* attains Brahman here (whilst still embodied); *Kena. Up.*, II.5 states, if Brahman is not known here in this life, greatest is the loss; *BU.*, III.8.10 states that he who passes from this world without *Brahma-jñāna* is the most pitiable, and, *Muṇḍ. U.*, III.2.9 states that the knower of Brahman himself becomes Brahman.

For Shankara, the doctrine of *jīvanmukti* is most important, for without its possibility there can be no genuine teacher of *Vedānta*. Besides, the factual evidence of Brahma-realisation will not be

[1] K.H. Potter, *EIP, Ch. U.B.*, p. 25; *B.G.B.*, XVIII.66.

possible. Besides, the great truth of the *Gītā* in the interest of a *jñāni* will not be forthcoming. Again, for the moderners, the possibility of a saintly saved life will be deemed to be a distant dream.

Inspite of the great value of *jīvanmukti* for Advaitism, this theory has been criticised both by the followers of Advaitism like Prakāśānanda and Sarvajñātamuni and Viśiṣṭādvaitin like Vedāntadeśika. In *Śatadūṣani*, Vada 31, Vedāntadeśika writes that after Brahma-realisation no embodiment is possible, and, if one is embodied then it means that he still has not been relased. The reason is that ignorance (which gives rise to body) and *jñāna* are absolutely opposed, and, so body cannot continue on the dawning of *Brahma-jñāna*, just as nightmare vanishes on awakening.

Here the views of Maṇḍana Mishra is worth-mentioning. According to Maṇḍana, *Brahma-jñāna* leads to the destruction of *Sañcita and prārabdha karmas* which means the immediate fall of the body terminating in *Videha-mukti*. Hence, according to Maṇḍana, there is no possibility of *jīvanmukti* in the sense of Shankara. For Shankara, the body continues as a result of the non-exhaustion of *prārabdha karma*, even though the body is now only a shadow of its avidyaic existence or just like a burnt out rope. This is in accordance with *Ch. U.*, VI.14.2, "For him (the *jñāni*) there is just this much delay, until he is not released, then he attains (liberation)." According to Maṇḍana, what Shankara calls a *jīvanmukta* is really a case of an advanced stage of *Sādhaka* (seeker). Most probably the contention of Shankara and Maṇḍana is not very substantial. Even Shankara would regard *Videhamukti* to be perfect only after the fall of the body.[1] Hence, the term of advanced '*Sādhaka*' and '*jīvanmukta*' really mean one and the same thing. But the orthodox Shankarites would not admit this, for according to Shankara, body continues for some time due to the residue of *avidya* in the same way in which after-image continues even when the stimulus has been withdrawn or the fan continues to move as a result of past motion even when the electric current has been withdrawn. Dr. Nalinikant Brahma in *The Philosophy of Hindu Sadhana*, pp. 189-91, mentions three views with regard to the continuance of the body for some time till the *prārabdha karma* is exhausted.

[1] *Vs.*, III.3.32; IV.1.15, 19; *B.G.B.*, XVIII.66; J. Kattackal, *Religion and Ethics in Advaita*, pp. 138-39, also p. 144, note 38; Shankara repeats that for a *jīvanmukta* there is delay till the body falls, *Ch. U.B.*, VI.14.2; K.H. Potter, *EIP*, *Brahmasiddhi*, p. 408-9.

1. The body continues for some time only as a result of *prārabdha karma*, even when *avidya* totally ceases.
2. According to others, with *Brahma-jñāna*, the concealing power of *avidya* is destroyed, but its power of super-imposition lasts for some time.
3. According to still some others notably Maṇḍana, ignorance does not cease wholly, even when, its power of deluding the *Brahma-jñānī* ceases altogether.

All these views agree that in some respects, ignorance continues even after *Brahma-jñāna:** only its effectiveness is destroyed. The highest knowledge i.e., *Brahma-jñāna* is not the means but is the liberation itself. Whatever be the activity of the body of the *jīvanmukta*, it has no binding effect. Only *sakāma karmas* have binding effects, but *niṣkāma karmas* are just as good as no *karmas* at all. They become totally transmuted and transvaluated by *Brahma-jñāna*. First, in the language of Sāṃkhya, *Brahma-jñānī* knows that he is non-agent (*a-kartā*) because Prakṛti with its guṇas is the real doer of acts.

> "And he really sees, who sees all actions being done in all respects only by Nature, and the self as the non-doer." (*B.G.*, XIII.29; also XIV.19).

Again, the *Brahma-jñānī* is said to rise above the three guṇas (*B.G.*, XIV.26). Thus, the *Brahma-jñānī* lives *in* the world, without being of the world. He gets rid of the illusoriness of the illusory world.

Such an emancipated man is not tormented by the thought of good and evil of his past actions (*Tait. U.*, II.9). He ceases to be a thief, a destroyer of an embryo or of being a *cāṇḍāla* (*B.U.*, IV.3.22). But it will be wrong to suppose that a *jīvanmukta* can perform evil or immoral action, as G.A. Jacob supposes. The reason is that self-control and resistance against all evils and temptations become a second nature of the *jīvanmukta*. Can a sage behave like a dog who returns to his vomit? (*Naiṣkarmyasiddhi*, IV.62, 63, 66, 68). One for whom there is nothing else to achieve and for whom all objects cease to have any meaning can perform no action, what to speak of any immoral action.

*This is specially maintained by Madhusudan who thinks that some remnant of *avidya* continues even in the highest stage of *jīvanmukti*, Jacob Kattackal, *Religion and Ethics in Advaita*, p. 195.

Of course, all past immoral acts are burnt up by knowledge. They disappear altogether. But can a *jīvanmukta* still having a body with *B-jñāna* not evil? No, why? Because

> " . . . . wrong perceptions do not arise in a man of realisation, for there is then no object for them." (*B.U.B.*, 1.4.10).

The point is that a saint can perform no evil action, just as a modern civilised man can hardly be expected to commit theft; or a *jīvanmukta* goes beyond social morality and rituals. (*B.U.B.*, II.3. 48) for society and the world cease to have any meaning for him. He becomes passionless and without desires. In the absence of motivation, he is as good as an inactive catatonic person. Besides, if he does any social action, then it cannot but be good. Why? Because as fragrance is natural to a rose, so good 'works or virtues become a part of second nature to him' (Sureshvarācārya's *Naiṣkarmya-siddhiḥ* IV.69). Not he but the eternal spirit breathes in him. His works cease to have any temporal effects, because they have to be viewed as *subspecie aeternitatis*. But it must be confessed that even the doctrine of *Sarvamukti* which came to be recognised in Advaitism and that of Bodhisattva in Budhism does not support secularism. The reason is simple. Secularism, strictly speaking is this worldly and liberation pertains to the supernatural or transcendental realm. Shankara at times suggests (*Vs.*, III.3.32) that a *jīvanmukta*, like the Bodhisattvas can return to the world in the service of humanity. But Maṇḍana, as Kuppusvami suggests, is opposed to this view.

3

The Modern Relevance of Shankara

The most important commitment of Shankara was to find out the way out of human miseries involved in earthly existence. Ontologically he established that the supreme reality is Brahman, which is eternal, unchangeable and untouched by the vicissitudes of any existents. After giving an ontological reason and defence of non-dual Brahman he proceeded to offer his epistemological explanation for the identity of knowing and being. The important contention is that the knower of Brahman himself becomes Brahman. The advaitic analysis of perception is that perception is possible when the *vṛttis* assume the shape and form of the objects cognized. Similarly by knowing Brahman, the knower himself becomes what he intuits of what Brahman is. Of course, this *gnosis* has to be occasioned by the moral and yogic discipline. Further, by knowing Brahman everything else is known, since it is the ground of every existent (jīvas and the things of the world). The very search of the Upanishadic seers was *kasmin nu vijñāte sarvam idam vijñātam bhavati*, and thereby by knowing Brahman and becoming Brhaman, one leaves behind the vale of miseries and enters into the bliss of Brahman.

Of course there is the difficulty in explaining the relationship between the phenomenal and noumenal entities. If Brahman remains wholly unaffected by worldly things, then how are the two related? The two are wholly unrelated according to *analogia entis* of Thomas Aquinas, Paul Tillich and also according to Shankara. However, Thomas Aquinas and Paul Tillich do not take recourse to illusionism. They hold that somehow through analogical (Aquinas) or symbolical ways (Tillich), we can reach very dimly the unconditioned Transcendent God. Paul Tillich is aware of the problem and ultimately comes to realise that the Transcendent Reality is 'God above God' which is not a place which one can reach. It is without the safety of words and concepts, without a name, a church, a cult or theology.[1] Why this *neti, neti* of every analogy and symbol?

The reason is that in having the *gnosis* of the Transcendent Brahman, one leaves behind the empirical world, the categories of thought and language. Consequently no talk about Brahman is possible; 'whereof one cannot speak, one should be silent'. But this is very significant 'silence', for one has to seek it with one's utmost diligence and seriousness. The discipline is once again physicolethical and religious.

Shankara resorts to the doctrine of *Ajñāna* or māyā to explain the relationship with the empirical and the transcendent reality of Brahman. Shankara is fully aware of the difficulties in describing the nature of māyā. He calls it indescribable (*sadasad vilakṣaṇa*). Its falsity is realised by working in, through and beyond it. When once one reaches the state of Brahma-realisation, one finds the utter irrelevance of the world, the scriptural learning and the ladder of *mahāvākyas*. Once the seeker understands the purport of *mahāvākyas*, he would recognize them as nonsensical as Wittgenstein would say. But climbing on, over and beyond the ladder of Vedāntic propositions is not an easy task. It is a difficult task, but all ultimate achievements are as difficult as they are rare. The superiority of Indian *gnosis* lies in the fact that the pathways have been fully marked and mapped out for us.

According to Shankara as also for Jainism and Buddhism, one has to use yogic and ethical technique along with knowledge imparted to by a competent Guru in order to have Brahma-realisation. One does not find any such technique elsewhere. But does one find Brahman? At the analogous stage of Guṇasthana in Jainism, one does not get any opportunity of uttering anything whatsoever. Thus here too one passes into silence. But to bring home the lesson of Brahma-realisation, Shankara refers to three paradigm cases of Brahma-like experience, namely, *nirvikalpaka pratyakṣa* (indefinite, vague, blur-like initial perception), *suṣupti* (dreamless sleep) and *turiya* (a yogic experience). Rāmānuja has criticized all these paradigm cases, and to my knowledge very correctly. The initial stage of perception is not without differences, but has incipient differences not yet parted into articulate relation, as was held by F.H. Bradley. The state of *suṣupti* is also not a state without dreams, but a state of forgotten dreams on awakening, as Sigmund

[1]*The Courage To Be*, p. 182.

Freud has amply demonstrated. Of course, *turiya* is a matter of yogic experience and discipline, as such beyond the purview of ordinary discourse. Keeping to the stand of Rāmānuja, in relation to ordinary language and its syntax, there can be no mental state corresponding to a case of pure *cit*. There is an analogous case of a sensum in relation to which no objective fact can be ostensibly demonstrated. Is it then an objection with regard to the theory of Brahman? No. If Brahma-realisation is a fact then certainly it cannot be factually demonstrated in terms of ordinary experience and language. It is a place without speech; it is a state of silnece. Any talk about Brahman will end in metaphysical heresy, an *avyakṛta* as Lord Buddha has pointed out.

Brahman is a matter of enlightenment, realisation and intuition. This has to be mediated through ethico-yogic discipline along with metaphysico-theistic discipline. Of course, for Shankara all these disciplines of yoga, morality and devotion are inseparable, as the *Gitā* too has upheld. Morality for Shankara may be described as striving for perfection by realising a state of desirelessness and egolessness. But this desideratum of moral ideal can be reached by the Vedāntic instruction of *nitya-anitya-vastuviveka*, *sādhanā-sampat* etc. and later on through *śravaṇa-manana-nididhyāsana*. In this context, one finds that Shankara does not mention theistic worship as a means of Brahma-realisation. Shankara does not mention God, for he is trying to bring home the importance of Brahma-realisation through Vedāntic discipline as distiniguished from theistic worship. But does not the distinction of *nitya-anitya* objects, indirectly refer to the different degrees of reality, including the highest phenomenal existence of Īshvara? Again, does not the teaching of *shama-dama-sādhanā-sampat* refer to Īshvara-worship through which alone *niṣkāma karma* and self-control are possible? But apart from this, we have already seen that Shankara accepts the path of devotion as a powerful aid in Brahma-realisation. The reason is that *Gītā* teaches that desirelessness in the form of *niṣkāma karma* is possible only when duties are performed as offerings to the Lord. This is very akin to what Kant had suggested that one should perform one's duties as God's command. The difference is that Kant regards morality as autonomous. Hence, the doctrine of treating duties as God's command remains extraneous to the main teaching of Kant. In contrast, the *Gītā* teaches morality as an in-built element in its theism.

Relativity of Deities

For Shankara, Brahman alone is real and all other deities are phenomenal, dependent and contingent. Therefore, they are not ultimately real. As dependent on Brahman they may be said to be relatively real. Again, *Yogasūtras* regard *upāsana* (*Īśavara-praṇidhāna*) as an aid for the success of yogic *sādhanā*. Similarly, following the *Gītā*, Shankara regards the worship of Īshvara as an aid for securing *Brahma-jñāna*. But Shankara significantly observes that the worship of Īshvara has many other ends besides the attainment of *B-jñāna*. Whilst commenting on *B.G.B.*, IV.11, Shankara observes that theistic worship is not directly related to *B-jñāna*. Following the *Gītā* it can be said that worshippers seek various kinds of fruits, and, the Lord grants their wishes if they worship their respective deities with full devotion. Some seek *B-jñāna*, others seek the gift of *niṣkāma karma*, and still others who are renunciate and *Vedānta-jñānin* seek *mokṣa*. Besides, the *Gītā* teaches that even the worshippers of the highest deity, namely, the Lord Krishna worship Him at times tamasically (XVII.4). This kind of worship will not lead to *B-jñāna* in any case. Further, Shankara does not hold Īshvara to be ultimately realy (*Vs.*, I.1.24; II.1.2.21; III.3.1). Consequently, Īshvara-worship has not been taken by Shankara as an infallible means of attaining *B-jñāna*. From this it does not follow that theism is not an important part of Shankara's Advaitism. In the last resort for Shankara all deities from the lowest to the highest have to be left behind and discarded on attaining Brahma. This means that there is an hierarchy of deities.

Certainly Shankara follows the *Gītā* and Gauḍapāda in their teaching of the hierarchy of gods. Gauḍapāda teaches the relativity and grades of different deities in championing the worship of *Om*, consisting of the four alphabets of *a*, *u*, *m* and the *amatra*. '*a*' stands for *Viśva*, '*u*' for *Taijasa* and '*m*' for *Prājña*. The worship of the three kinds of deities prepares the seeker for the final stage of *amatra*, that is, the state in which all the deities disappear in *Brahma-jñāna*. The worship of *Viśva* gives worldly success to his worshippers, but these worshippers remain fettered to the existence of Saṃsāra. The worshippers of *Taijasa* get the urge for higher knowledge attaining which leads to a state in which all persons are treated alike, including enemies and friends (*MKB.*, I.10). But the worship of *Prājña* (Īshvara) stands highest in the order of worship, involving dualism. But every form of dualism belongs to the realm of impirical reality. Īshvara worship can lead to heavenly bliss and beatitude. However, the heavenly abode is temporary and one has to get back to the worldly existence after the store of merits has been exhausted. For having eternal deliverance one must obtain *B-jñāna*. The worship of Īshvara prepares one for *B-jñāna* for Īshvara enables a worshipper to conquer his possions and desires, and, mitigate the influence of ignorance, for the Lord is the controller of māyā. But in the end it is meditation on *amatra*, which alone leads to B-realisation.

It is not open to every one to worship any kind of deity. What kind of deity a worshipper will choose depends on the kind of person he is. In other words, it depends on the *saṃskāras*, and in the language of C.G. Jung, on one's typology, mental functioning and constitution. Three kinds of *saṃskāra* have been mentioned, namely, *sāttvika, rājasika* and *tāmasika*. *Sāttvika* people worship the gods, *rājasika* the demi-gods and the *tāmasika* worship the spirits and ghosts (*B.G.*, XVII.4). Thus the kind of deity corresponds to the typology of the seeker, because the two are attuned to each other. Whe an appropriate object of worship attuned to the mentality of the worshipper is presented then it clicks life and light in him, gives him energy and strength to him for the task in which he is involved. If, on the other hand, the deity does not correspond to his mental proclivities, then the worshipper remains cold to it. Nay, more. Even the highest deity will be used in accordance with the *saṃskāra* of the worshipper. For example, a worshipper of Krishna or Christ may use his religion for worldly benefit if his *saṃskāra* is *tāmasika*. Thus each religion can be used in the way in which its worshippers are psychologically constituted.

Hence, there must be different religions and deities corresponding to different kinds of persons are (psychologically constituted). In vain, we teach the universality of any theistic worship either of Rama or Krishna or Christ. No theistic religion has the monopoly of religious truth. Each person is condemned to his own *saṃskāras*, which work as his fate. But each dualistic worship is valid since it alone click life and light, peace and *pistis* to its votaries. Thus each form of theism is valid, and yet cannot claim precedence over all the rest. In the end every form of dualistic worship has to serve as an aid for *B-jñāna*. Therefore, each form of theism is both true empirically and yet false transcendentally. Accepting spiritual fatalism of *saṃskāras*, called the doctrine of pre-destination and election by Ajivikism, Christianity and Islam, there is hardly any room for quarrel between the different votaries of various religions.

Shankara teaches that each form of dualistic worship is ultimately false. So each is infected with the spirit of its transcendence, pointing the way to Brahma-realisation, were every form of theism terminates. In the language of the *Gītā,* the lower forms of worship end in the worship of the absolute Lord (*B.G.*, VII.21-23). Shankara goes one step further, for according to him, even the worship of Lord Krishna must be transcended at the final stage of Brahma-realisation. In *B-jñāna* alone, all differences cease, and there is no room for discord:

> "There a father becomes not a father; a mother, not a mother; the worlds, not the worlds; the gods, not the gods; . . . ." (*Bṛhadāraṇyaka U.*, IV.3.22).

In this connection Shankara states thus:

> ". . . . the aim of the Shāstra is to discard all distinctions fictitiously created by Nescience." (*Vs.*, I.1.4, p. 32).

This is the absolute standard and there can be nothing higher. We go beyond the world into the region of 'silence', according to Shankara, Buddhism and Wittgenstein. We can reach this stage by systematically denying the lower forms of theistic worship. Each God has to be worshipped and yet finally denied in our upward march towards the ascent of differenceless Brahman. Hence, according to the *Gītā*, Gauḍapāda and Shankara, the hierarchical arrangement of different deities explains the inherent principle of self-transcendence, iconoclasm, atheistic and protestant principle in each form of dualistic worship. Even Paul Tillich could not give any better rationale of the protestant principle. Wittgenstein was not thinking about different religions, but he also admitted that even the highest kind of scientific knowledge is stilled in the speechless silence about God, Who is wholly indescribable. Indeed Shankara seems supreme in his absolute iconoclasm of lower deities. This works wonderfully in relation to the Indian scene, of today.

The highest form of theism is of the devotional kind. Each devotee gives himself wholly without any reserve to the service of the Lord. The Lord in turn remains the sole refuge and reality of His devotees. Yet with all its beauty and grandeur a Shivite will persecute a Vaiṣṇava, and a Vaiṣṇava in turn will look down upon other votaries of different gods. Hence, even the highest form of theism cannot but give way to discord and dissension. This is seen in the conflict between the Roman Catholics and Pratestants in Ireland, between the Muslims and Christians in Lebanon, between the votaries of various forms of theism in India.

Whichever be the form of theism, there is always the dualism of the worshipper and his God. This dualism leads to idolatry and discord. It leads to discord: a Christian would say that Jesus is Īshvara, a Vaiṣṇava would say Krishna or Viṣṇu is Īshvara ond so on. Each and every monotheist is worshipping one and the same God, yet they all differ because of different names and forms, leading to religious strife and bloodshed.

Are Īshvara, Viṣṇu, Krishna, Christ, Shiva one and the same name of God? In one sense it is so, since they ultimately refer to the same underlying referent behind these names of Gods. But in another sense they fail to refer to the same underlying reality. For instance, Krishna and Christ are different pictures, with their different stories, eliciting different commitments of their respective adherents. But they are both symbols, participating in and pointing to Brahman, which transcends all symbols. Following Paul Tillich we can say that no symbol can take the place of the Unconditioned Brahman. If we fail to treat the symbols as but symbols of the absolute Brahman, we commit idolatry. We have to reach 'God beyond God'. In the language of Shankara, even the highest religious symbol must be left behind like the ladder which has to be left behind on reaching Brahman from which there is no further possibility of returning to the miserable existence of earthly life. This is as much applicable to Christianity as to Hindu Theism.

Jesus said, 'I and my father are one', and the again, 'My father is greater than myself'. Colossian I.15 says that Christ is the visible image of the invisible God, and, that 'nobody has seen God and can ever see Him' (1 Timothy VI.16). The conclusion is that we can apprehend or intuit the invisible, qualityless Being-itself or Brahman through the symbol of Jesus. But it would be an idolatry not to recognize Jesus as but representation only, of Brahman. Thus, every form of theism has to break through its idolatry in its forward march towards Brahman. How is it to be achieved?

Wittgenstein has stated that in every form of theism, the most important thing is the picture. He clearly states that this picture does not point to anything which exists. In the language of Paul Tillich, Being-itself is beyond essence (thought, idea and existence; and, for Nāgārjuna, it is Shūnyatā. But we mortals draw picture, as the sage Nāgasena had to do for king Milinda in relation to exhibiting the form of Nirvana. We know that beauty does not exist, only beautiful things exist. Yet for the articulation of beauty, the picture of Venus has been painted. Botticelli, Veronese, Titian, Boucher, Raoux and so on have all painted 'Venus'. Of course, it would be irrelevant to say that any one of them is the true Venus. Venus is not the existing Miss Universe. Yet one can say that some of them bring out the delineation of feminine beauty more sharply than others. In the same way, we draw a picture of Brahman which is the ground of all beings. In the light of our advancing knowledge, finer susceptibilities and ever deepening-growing-widening sensitiveness to our spiritual dimension of life, we keep on improving upon our symbols or pictures. Like Leonardo, we keep on improving the painting of the mysterious Mona Lisa. Take the case of Yahwe.

For the Jews Yahwe was at first only a tribal God of storm and thunder. Then later on He became a God of gods. It was prohibited to have any image of him for fear of idolatry. But He could be appeased through animal sacrifice. This picture was later on chiselled into a God who desires mercy and a contrite heart, and not the sweet savour of sacrifice. Finally, Yahwe came to stand for a loving and forgiving God who transforms the life of a sinner through the redemptive death of Jesus Christ.

Hence the name remains but the picture gets chiselled and refined through the ages as a result of growing spiritual sensitiveness of the worshippers. This refinement by discarding the older picture is the negative way of *analogia entis*, the atheistic principle of Paul Tillich; *neti, neti* of the *Upanishads* and Shankara and the negativating dialectic or Bradley and Nāgārjuna. But how far should we keep on refining the picture? There is no limit. Shankara would say that Brahman is the absolute limit beyond which we cannot go. Nāgārjuna would say that even the indescribable Brahman described substantively must not be set up as the limit. Shūnyatā the way of dialectic negation is the only safe limit. Should we listen to Shankara or Nāgārjuna?

We transcend the empirical thought in reaching the goal of Brahman or Shūnyatā. The 'yes' and 'no' are the two extremes of the final limit between which our thought oscillates, and, in this oscillation the seeker plumbs one's depth. Saying anything beyond this is to commit the metaphysical heresy, to which Lord Buddha has drawn our attention. But is this the counsel of despair? No.

The drawing of a picture of something which does not exist and yet is the most real thing which underlies all that exists, has very great value for the Indians. According to this insight of Shankara and Paul Tillich, no theistic form can calm the sole monopoly of religious truth. Each form of theism has only relative truth and stands in need of being supplemented by the relative insights of the same reality contained in other theistic forms. Hence, this thought of Shankara calls forth for a true dialogue amongst all forms of theism in the hope that each religion will cross-fertilizes the thoughts of every other forms of theism. This mutual dialogue and cross-fertilization will make each form of theism refine its own picture of what it considers to be the Most Holy. The result?

Religions will outgrow their mutual hate and arrogance. This is possible when each form of dualistic worship will recognize its limitation and also the supreme need to reach the sphere of the silence of Brahman where all discords and differences cease to be effective. In this supreme state of *Silence*, a Muslim will not be a Muslim, a Hindu will not be a Hindu, a Christian will not continue to be a Christian. All names, forms and labels will disappear, all different pots called 'you' and 'me' will get broken, all differences will melt into a grand harmony. This is a general conclusion. But more.

In every form of dualistic worship, difference will tend to be slurred over. A Christian pervaded with the spirit of Shankara will not recognize the difference of race, culture, regions, language and denominations. It is not an easy thing to achieve in practice. Southern Christians of Kerala observe caste (differences to Brahmins and Shudras) in church worship. They have separate churches of worship and even separate cemeteries. Again, in spite of one Church of North India, Anglicans and churches belonging to other denominations continue to have their own mode of worship. Similarly, Malayalis and Adivasis have their own separate mode of worship and priests. If the Christians cannot become one then how can they then expect to promote national integration and the unity of all religions? But let us come to Hinduism from where we have picked the absolute principle of differencelessness into which all religious dialogues end.

Can a Hindu clinging the *Atman*-principle of Shankara accept caste and sects? It will not do to say that the case observances will automatically cease in*B-jñāna*, for no *B-jñāna* will ever dawn till we begin to show and feel strongly that caste is ultimately false, like all other differences. First, it is based on a single *Ṛgvedic* hymn of Purusha-sūkta (*Rv.*, 90). Secondly, it has been criticized at its inception by no less a person than Lord Buddha.[1]

1. Lord Buddha observed that people belonging to different castes have the same biological, anatomical and physiological characteristics. So why differentiate between the people when as human beings they belong to the same species of living beings?
2. By birth there is no Brahman and Shudra: only one's works determine one's vocation and social order.
3. Spiritually speaking, there is the same uniform law of righteousness and the same kind of punishment on its violation.
4. It is the economic status which makes one person the master and the other as his servant.
5. Caste is not a universal order, for even in Lord Buddha's time in Kamboja (present Afghanistan) there was no caste.

From the very nature of the case, caste is indefensible for a Brahma-seeker. A *Brahma-jñānī*, if he offers his leavings to an outcaste, then it is really an offering to his universal *Atman* (*Ch. U.*, V.24.4). Again, a *Brahma-jñānī* makes on difference between a Brahmin and an outcaste (*Gītā*, V.18). Besides, for a *jīvanmukta* there is no difference between his father and others, between a god and a cāṇḍāla (*Bṛhad. U.*, IV.3.22). Finally, Brahman, Itself has no caste. (*Muṇḍ. U.*, I.1.6).

True, Shankara himself observed caste, but he belonged to AD 788-820 when there was no Darwin, and no Industrial Revolution and the economic order of the present time. He was a product of his age. But does the doctrine of *B-jñāna* support his observance of caste? Shankara denied the right of a Shudra for *B-jñāna*, for according to his statement Vedic learning is a necessary preparation

[1]*Majjhima Nikāya,* Hindi tr. by Rāhula Sāṅkṛtyāyana. *Sutta-Nipata*, Chulla-vagga, pp. 72-79, *Vaseṭṭha Sutta* in Mahavagga, pp. 58-173.

for *B-jñāna* and a Shudra is debarred from the studies of the *Vedas*. But does Shankara subscribe to the efficacy of Vedic *Karmakāṇḍa*? Shankara does not see any good in the performance of Vedic *Karmakāṇḍa*. Hence, really Shankara's Advaitism does not support caste. If we follow the spirit and not the letter, then caste will appear as inconsistent with Shankara's Advaitism.

Therefore, a Brahman-seeker must outgrow caste-distinction in the interest of *B-jñāna* and for promoting national integration and for the preservation of Hinduism in its purest form for the spiritual good of India and the world. Further, the doctrine of differenceless Brahman has another practical consequence on the Indian scene in relation to different sects in Hinduism and the misuse of religion.

According to the *Gītā* (XVII.4) men belong to different types and mentality, according to their guṇas and *saṃskāra*. In accordance with their typology, men worship the kind of deity open to their mental proclivities. Further, in accordance with their devotion to their respective deities, they get their reward. However, keeping to the hierarchical order involved in the worship of *Om*, one has to rise from the lower to the highest deity till he reaches a stage where all deities disappear. Hence, there must be various religions and sects even in the same religion. Thus every theistic religion has to practise tolerance of different religions and sects.

But apart from this there is a great danger of the misuse of religion. Ordinarily, the worship of Īshvara is for the *sāttvika* people. But even the *tāmasika* people can pretend to worship Īshvara, and if they do so, they can do that only tamasically. Here the highest Lord will come to be worshipped for worldly gain and pleasures. Whereas, according to Shankara, Īshvara should be worshipped properly only for the sake of realising *B-jñāna* where all differences of caste and creed are swallowed up. No doubt the *tāmasika* worshipper of Īshvara will get worldly prosperity and power (*Gītā*, VII.21) but is does not mean that it is either good for him or for the country. Shankara teaches constant vigilance in promoting the spiritual health of the people. By trivializing the worship of Īshvara, there will be chaos in the country, as we find it today.

Shankara's philosophy of a world religion is good enough even now, since it is supported by the modern thinkers like Paul Tillich and Luding Wittgenstein. But times have changed and even the great thought of Shankara requires restatement in the changed climate of thought and world-view. Shankara was the ripened fruit of the spiritual quest enshrined in the four-fold pillars of *karma-samsāra-jñāna-mukti*. The Indian people believed in them by practising austerities and *sannyāsa*. This is supported by the Greek report about the Indians about 300 BC.[1] Do the modern Indians believe in them? Take the case of the doctrine of *sarvamukti* (salvation for all).

The doctrine of *sarvamukti* is implicit in the universal teaching of deliverance in the *Upanishads*. Even in the Advaitism Vācaspati it is implicit, and, Appaya Dikṣita explicitly taught this and so did Radhakrishnan in 1932. Again, in the doctrine of Bodhisattvas, the ideal of *sarvamukti* is quite explicit. The result? Nirvana for the vast majority is as distant a dream as it was in the days of Lord Buddha. Further, a *jivanmukta* was supposed to be a beacon-light who will draw the whole world towards himself.

> 'Whatever a great man does, the same is done by others also. Whatever standard he sets, the world follows.' (*Gitā*, III.21).

Unfortunately the society has not been drawn towards the *jīvanmukta*. The people praise a *jīvanmukta;* even idolise him, but they donot follow him. There is hardly a Brahmavid today, and hardly a follower of Buddha tries to become a Buddha today. Why?

First, Shankara in *Bhaja Govindam* shows that mental equipose is a rare achievement for even a gifted seeker. What to speak for the masses? But the truth is that the modern Indians do not look upon the world as a vale of miseries. They do not want *mukti*, though the way has been clearly laid down. The moderners do not want the extinction of their egos. They desire the expansion and enrichment of their ego-consciousness. What about the society in which a man lives?

Certainly the ancients were ignorant of the societal changes and their dynamics. The advaitins believed in the preservation and conservation of the society based on the system of caste. They were conservatives in our political terms. Even Shankara and Rāmānuja accepted the doctrine of caste without realising its divisive and exploitative functions. Certainly, the system of caste has preserved

[1]J.W. McCrindle, *Ancient India*, pp. 168-70.

the Hindu society. But today we need progress much more than the preservation of an old and tattered society. As Shankara did not believe in progress, so he has no programme of social service.

For Shankara, the empirical world was illusory and essentially miserable. Hence, for Shankara the world did not require any improvement. As such Shankara had no programme of alleviating social ills and human miseries. In contrast, the moderners regard the world as essentially real. They want the improvement in the human conditions of living. As Shankara did not pay much attention to Nature and its possible use for reducing drudgeries, so he did not recommend the conquest of nature with a view to improving socio-economic conditions of man. Of course the time was not ripe for the conquest of nature. Science in the form of a cooperative effort of man backed by social resources, and regulated by its rigorous methodology, had not arisen. Only now with the help of science and its technology it is possible for man to conquer nature. Would Shankara at the present time in our modern context recommend the doctrine of *karma-sannyāsa*? In my opinion the views of Shankara would change considerably. But this is anybody's guess. Shankara has said this much that the world has phenomenal reality, and as long as individuals do not obtain *B-jñāna*, they have to treat the world as real with its demands. Only he would add, 'Dedicate the fruits of scientific pursuit to the Lord.'

Would Shankara recommend *Karma-Jñāna-Samuccayavāda* of Maṇḍana and Rāmānuja? Of course, this *samuccayavāda* is quite opposed to the principle of *B-jñāna* leading to the realisation and enjoyment of differenceless Brahman. Further, '*karma*' for Maṇḍana and Rāmānuja meant only the Vedic ritual and sacrifice. And this kind of *karma* is not likely to contribute to social well-being. Further, the doctrine of *lokasamgraha* simply meant the conservation of the society on the basis of caste. Hence, *Karma-Jñāna-Samuccayavāda* would not serve the purposes of the moderners. Whatever be the emendations in Advaitism, Shankara certainly would recommend science and technology as offerings to the Lord. Science and technology, nay, even the conquest of nature are not enough. Their pursuit must be spiritualised. The words of Maitreyi are true even now.

> What should I do with that through which I may not be immortal? (*BU.*, II.4.3).

The path of spiritual ascent is never straight. Any advance in spiritual progress is always threatened with back-sliding. Man's life oscillates between engagement with the world and withdrawal from it. Spiritual progress is a matter of dialectical process as Nāgārjuna has demonstrated for us. The present crisis on the Indian scene is a grim reminder of the fall of man from what he was at the time of Lord Buddha, Lord Mahavira and Shankara. In our spiritual pilgrimage there is no place where we can rest for ever. There may be resting places, but there can be no final goal. This is the meaning of *neti, neti.*

Some Implications of Shankara's Advaitism

In the light of what has been stated by Shankara, Paul Tillich and Wittgenstein, some very significant conclusions can be drawn. Let us take up a very popular question, Does God exist?

God as understood as Brahman or Being-itself is beyond māyā, beyond existence and human thought. As such He cannot be said to exist. Only a sensible, finite thing is said to exist. But Brahman or Being-itself is not unreal or fictitious. It is the ground of all that exists. Īshvara or the God of theistic worship is a picture or symbol of Brahman, participating in and pointing to the reality of Brahman. However, even a symbol is psychologically, phenomenally and practically real as long as *B-jñāna* has not dawned. God, even as a symbol has to be worshipped.

Further, a picture of Brahman in the form of Rāma, Krishna and Christ is associated with stories called mythologies. For instance, Īshvara is said to be the creator of the world and the determiner of human destiny in accordance with the past *karmas* of each jīva. In the same way Lord Krishna and Christ are associated with the story of saving sinners. These stories, according to R.B. Braithwaite, have empirical meaning. But can Jesus or Buddha even with the stories be said to exist?

A series of symbols strung up into stories is called mythology. If a mythology is woven round a historical figure like Jesus or Lord Buddha, then their respective votaries take both the stories and them as existing beings. But to the extent these historical figures existed, they cannot be spiritually significant for us. As historical persons, they are dead and gone. However, as eschatological figures they continue to be efficacious in the lives of their worshippers. Hence, as deities they cannot be said to exist. But they are real in the sense that they are effective in transforming the lives of their votaries. Take another instance of world-creation. Has Īshvara actually created the universe?

'Creation' is only an analogical concept. For knowing how the world has come into being, one has to consult the scientsis, astronomers etc. Hence, the religious doctrine of 'world-creation' is not a scientific doctrine. It is analogical, symbolical and pictorial. For theistic believers, it has only an existential meaning. Since God has created the world, he will sustain His creatures in the face of threat of non-existence. But what about the claims of the Christian fundamentalists concerning the *Bible?*

The fundamentalists believe that the *Bible* is an exact replica of the original which is in heaven. This language is only mythological. In the language of Shankara and Wittgenstein, even the advaitic philosophy and scripture are māyika ladders which have to be set aside after one has realised the ultimate truth through them. But this teaching is fraught with danger if we do not fully understand this doctrine of Shankara.

Of course, according to Shankara, Īshvara is only māyika and has to be finally denied on the attainment of *B-jñāna.* Hence, the half-educated people may think that the worship of Īshvara is fictitious and superstitious. Such people may declare that religion is an opiate of the masses, and is an illusion. But, according to Paul Tillich, even the mythology of one kind concerning God has to be set aside in favour of another mythology. Man cannot live without God, without some attendant mythology. What these people seek to deny is not the God of theistic worship, but the *tāmasika* use of religion. And the misuse of religion is quite discernible when we use it fanatically for gaining political gains. For this reason the advaitic thinkers did not like to teach their philosophy except to those persons who were fit for this kind of *jñāna.* This teaching was imparted only to those persons who were morally disciplined and psychologically prepared for *B-jñāna.*

Shankara knew well that even Īshvara could be worshipped tamasically, and not for the purpose of obtaining *mokṣa.* For this reason Shankara preferred his doctrine of *śravaṇa-manana-nididhyāsana* to the expedient of theistic worship for obtaining release. Shankara fully subscribed to the doctrine of *bhakti*, but he saw the danger of it. Shankara as such has remained the most devoted worshipper of Īshvara and yet at the same time the greatest critic of theism. Theistic worship without being informed by the advaitic principle of differenceless Brahman is fraught with dangers. Instead of bringing peace, it is likely to end in hate, strife and constant tension.

4

Theoretical Gains

Apart from the practical utility of Shankara's philosophy of Brahman, there is theoretical gain too. The religious philosophy of differenceless Brahman permits every form of theism if it is used in the service of Brahma-realisation. But if God be taken as an existent fact and religious statements as cognitive, then theistic statements get riddled with contradictions. Let us illustrate the points in the light of analytic philosophy.

From the time of Kant up to the present age, it is taken for granted that the so-called proofs for the existence of God are no proofs at all. They are simply pleas i.e., persuasive arguments. According to John Wisdom,[1] these arguments are neither deductive nor inductive. They are simply devout expressions of the believing theists. But as such they will not be regarded as cognitive. In the last thirty years or so, it has been shown that the very concept of God as an existent fact is self-contradictory or absurd.

J.N. Findlay has analysed the logic of worship and God as an adequate object of religious attitude.[2] According to his analysis, there are three notions which can be stated about God as an adequate object of religious worship.

1. God must be all comprehensive.
2. He must necessarily exist.
3. He must have all His attributes necessarily.

In other words, God as an adequate object of worship means to be a *necessary being*. But the very concept of a Necessary Being is self-contradictory. 'Necessary' can be used appropriately only for the statements where words are used consistently in their stipulated meanings e.g., mathematical statements. But certainly 'God' is not

[1]John Wisdom, *Gods*, Proceedings of Aristotelian Society, 1944-45.

[2]J.N. Findlay, 'Can God's Existence be Disproved?' in *New Essays in Philosophical Theology* (*NEPT*), ed. A. Flew and A. Macintyre.

a mere matter of words which have come into being through definitions like 'triangle' or 'straight line' that may or may not exist. However, if God be an existent Being, then no statement concerning a fact properly be called 'necessary'. Hence, the concept of God as a 'Necessary Being' is self-contradictory.

Many replies have been made by the philosophers in defence of the concept of a 'Necessary Being', which need not be taken up here. But Findlay forgets that not analysis of a fact can lead to a conclusion by *implication*. Worship of God is a psychological fact and worshippers need not draw a logical conclusion with regard to their object of worship. For example, Yahwe was just a tribal god and was considered to be one of the many other tribal gods. But the analysis of J.N. Findlay has a lesson for all those theologians who regard God as a 'Necessary Being'. Many sufterfuges in defence of the concept of 'Necessary Being' have not proved to be successful. Difficulties will arise if God be taken to be a fact and if God-talk be regarded as assertions. Let us illustrate this point with regard to the analysis of God-talk by A. Flew.

A. Flew in 'Theology and Falsification'[1] holds that if theistic statements are factual assertions, then like any other assertions they must be falsifiable. This criterion of falsifiability concering empirical propositions was developed by Kral Popper in the light of the remark by Einstein. Now Flew shows that a theistic statement like 'God is love' is not falsifiable for the following reasons:

1. The word like 'love' or 'wisdom' is killed by a thousand qualifications with the result that no state of affairs has any possibility of falsifying the statement 'God is love'.
2. Besides, a theist is so much committed to God that he will not count anything against the theistic statement 'God is love'.
3. When the actual state of affairs does not prove his point then a theist appeals to a metaphysical ground. According to this metaphysical basis the world as a whole, here and hereafter, alone can falsify any theistic assertion.

But if theistic assertions are not falsifiable then they are empirically vacuous and empty of any factual meaning. No satisfactory

[1]A, Flew, *NEPT*, pp. 96-108.

defence could be made against this conclusion of Flew, if theistic statements are taken to be factual assertions.[1]

When we begin to consider God's attributes of creatorship, omnipotence, infinitude etc., then we can fare no better if these concepts be used in their usual cognitive meanings. Take creatorship. If, God creates out of nothing, then He creates something out of nothing, which according to the *Chāndogya* is self-contradictory. If, however, He creates the world out of pre-existing matter etc., as in Nyāya-Vaiśeṣika schools, then God is reduced to the status of an architect as Shankara and Kant would say, and then, He ceases to be a creator. Again, J.L. Mackie shows that the very concept of 'omnipotence' is self-contradictory.[2] He puts a question, Can an omnipotent Being make rules which bind Him or create beings which he cannot subsequently control?

> "If we answer 'yes', it follows that if God actually makes things which he cannot control, or make rules which bind himself, he is not omnipotent once he has made them: there are *then* things which he cannot do. But if we answer 'No' we are immediately asserting that there are things which he cannot do, that is, to say that he is already not omnipotent."

In the same manner, A. Flew shows that the fact of evil in the world refutes God's omnipotence. Even the defence in terms of free will does not take one out of the crisis of evil in the world.[3]

Seeing that religious assertions cannot be cognitive, the contemporary thinkers have presented various expedients to get out of the impasser. For example, R.M. Hare thinks that religious statements are Blik statements, which view reminds one of the 'animal instinct' in man, according to Hume. Blik, according to R.M. Hare, does not *describe facts*, but expresses our *attitude* to facts,—a deep-seated attitude which is relatively stable and not easily upset by rational arguments. R.M. Hare has not explained the why of Blik, but we trust that it is explicable in terms of the holistic tendency in man to become full, entire and perfect. As Blik-theory is

[1]Interested reader may consult author's *Introduction to Religious Philosophy*, pp. 45-53.

[2]'Evil and Omnipotence' in *Mind*, 1955.

[3]J.L. Mackie, op. cit., p. 210.

purely suggestive and does not elaborate the nature of theistic statements, so we need not further discuss this.

Another thinker like R.M. Hare is R.B. Braithwaite. According to R.B. Braithwaite, religious statements are really moral statements backed by stories.[1] One need not believe in the factual truth of the story, but the story should consist in principle of empirical propositions.[2] Certainly religious stories are important for they present of logic of religious statements of any theistic religion. But religion is much more than morality. In the Indian context, the moral discipline is merely preparatory for obtaining religious insight, and, in the final ascent in religious pursuit one has to go even beyond 'what is good and evil'. None the less, the importance of stories has been accepted by Witgenstein to which reference has already been made. These stories, however are much more than merely empirical in principle and for there real nature we have to turn to R. Bultmann.

For a little over forty-five years, the Christian theologian R. Bultmann has declared that much of the New Testament language can be called mythological. According to him, the doctrine of virgin birth, resurrection, the three-storied structure of the univers etc., are to be regarded as mythological. What is true of Christianity is also applicable to some other forms of theism. But Bultmann's teaching about mythology and demythologising is as unsatisfactory as the Blik-theory of R.M. Hare and that of Braithwaite. The lesson from Bultmann's teaching is that the mythological stories of the *Bible* in their literal sense are not acceptable to the modern man, for these stories can be accepted only by the pre-scientific primitive mentality. Bultmann, however, failed to realise that any talk about the supernatural Being is bound to be mythic, for here we go beyond science and ordinary language. Only one has to find a proper myth suitable for a modern man. At the time when Bultmann was advancing his doctrine of demythologising the German people were believing in the myth of pure blood and swastika.

Thus we conclude that God cannot be taken to be an existent fact, for his concept is full of inner contradiction. But it is true to say that some kind of deity is indispensible for man so that through

[1] R.B. Braithwaite, 'An Empiricist's View of the Nature of Religious Belief' in *The Existence of God,* ed. John Hick, pp. 229-52.

[2] Ibid., p. 246.

his deity he may get attuned to the Supreme Power at the basis of the evolutionary process. This can be done when God is regarded as a symbol which was taught by Shankara in the past and has been adopted and advanced by Pul Tillich. At least this much is fact of the case that God cannot be regarded either as a cause or the metaphysical ground of the universe. As to the first point Hans Reichenbach writes:

> "The question of the cause of the first event, or of the cause of the universe as a whole is not a serious problem. The word 'cause' denotes a relation between two things and is inapplicable if only one thing is concerned. The universe as a whole has no cause, since by definition, there is nothing outside it that could be its cause. Questions of this sort are empty verbalism rather than philosophic agrument."[1]

This criticism of Reichenbach reminds one of the observation of Kant that the category of causality is applicable only to the phenomena but not to the noumena.

Again, J.A. Ayer too like Reichenbach regards the idea of the First Cause as absurd:

> '. . . . clearly on event can be prior to all of them; becauce if it is a member of the class of all of them it must be included in it, and therefore, can't be prior to it.'[2]

This criticism of A.J. Ayer reminds one of Russell's theory of Description according to which no level of language even that of metacausality applies to itself reflexively. Further, we have already noted that no meaning or explanation of the universe lies within the universe. Hence, God cannot be a member of the universe or an existing fact within the universe. And if one goes beyond the universe, then his language which has its legitimate use within the universe, cannot apply to God who goes beyond the universe. Hence any theistic deity can only be a symbol which takes us to the Transcendent Reality beyond the universe. However, if we take the transcendent to be a fact within the phenomena, then we fall

[1]*The Rise of Scientific Philosophy*, p. 280.
[2]MacGregor and Robb, *Readings in Religious Philosophy*, p. 334.

into antinomies, paralogisms and ideals of reason. This intellectual impasse should show that we reach here the utmost limit of our intellectual tether. We can talk only in symbols. In the language of Shankara, a symbol takes us into the presence of Brahman. Once we have reached our destination the symbol too ceases.

Hence we conclude that intellectual impasse with regard to God arises because we take God to be an existent being. The way out of the intellectual crisis is to see that God is nothing but a symbol of Brahman.

Shankara and Social Change

We have held in the very beginning that religion is a social phehomenon and implicitly we have maintained that Shankara's philosophy of theism paves the way for social peace and inter-religious dialogue. But some people object that Shankara's philosophy teaches *sannyāsa* for achieving one's spiritual goal. Should the philosophy of *sannyāsa* be accepted today by the moderners who have to remain highly involved in the world?

Shankara had the religious climate of the doctrine of *karma-saṃsāra-jñāna-mukti* and also of āshrama-dharmas. According to Shankara, everybody in his stage of studentship and householdership was not expected to take to *sannyāsa*. Only those persons who had the aptitude for attaining spiritual excellence were required to take to *sannyāsa*. This point was a matter of controversy between Shankara and Maṇḍana. Shankara would require everyone engaged in State and Public service to perform his duties in the spirit of the *Gītā* i.e., duties have to be performed as offerings to the Lord. Such offerings are pleasing to the Lord. And what will the Lord do? Quite obviously he would make a Shankarite seeker fit for Brahma-realisation. Hence, Shankara would not be against social service and progress. But why did not Shankara emphasize social service for the alleviation of human sufferings and uplift of the masses?

First, Shankara did not feel any need for this emphasis. Āshrama-dharmas were well known and were acceptable to the people of his time. Secondly, the social structure had become quite stable, and even the Buddhists who were opposed to caste and āshrama-dharmas were on the run. What could be the necessity for Shankara to take up the task of social change and progress? This explains the absence of any social philosophy in Shankara's thought. But did Shankara accept even his *sannyāsa* very rigidly? Did not Shankara perform the last rite of his mother which as a sannyāsi he was not expected to perform? Hence Shankara did show that āshrama-dharmas are made for man and not man for āshrama-dharmas. Shankara was certainly beyond his times even in relation to social duties. But one question can still be asked, 'Had Shankara lived in our time in modern India, would he still hold on to caste-distinction which has polluted so much of our whole democratic set-up and which is no longer acceptable to the Shudras and Adivasis?

It is anybody's guess. However, two points can be noted here. Swami Vivekananda was a modern advaitin. He did not accept caste. Secondly, he encouraged social service. Sankara would thank Swami Vivekananda for his services to the cause of Advaitism. We think that if Shankara were living today he would not accept caste, for Brahman itself has no caste and in Brahma-realisation caste-distinction disappears. Again, Shankara accepted the reality of the phenomenal world as long as *B-jñāna* does not dawn. He would say with Vivekananda:

> "Plunge into the world and learn the secret of work. Do not fly from the wheels of the world-machine. Should inside it and see how it functions. You can find a way to come out of it."[1]

[1]Quoted by V.S. Narvane, *Modern Indian Thought*, p. 206.

5

Summary and Conclusion

A. 1. Brahma is the sole reality.

2. The individuality of the jīvas and the diversities of the world are ultimately false, since they have only empirical reality.
3. The relation between Brahma and illusory individuality and diversity is itself illusory.
4. This doctrine of *Sadasat Ajñāna* does not require, any explanation with regard to its beginning. But one can use therapeutic Vedāntic knowledge for ending the miserable state of *ajñāna.*
5. Brahma remains unaffected by the vicissitudes in the life of the jīvas and ongoings of the world.
6. Brahma remains wholly undifferentiated and its realisation means the attainment of a state of *neti, neti* or silence, in which all differences of competing creeds are swallowed up.
7. This doctrine of reaching a state of differenceless Brahman has the practical import of reconciling all differences in religion, and, has also the merit of regulating each worshipper to overcome all differences within his own creed as a preparatory step for reaching the absolute state of Brahma-realisation.

B. The doctrine of Brahma-realisation is superior to its Western counterparts.

1. According to F.H. Bradley, ultimately thought working through the dualistic categories must commit a happy suicide in the harmony of the Absolute. But what about the appearances?

(a) No appearances are lost, but ultimately are re-absorbed after undergoing necessary transformation.

> "Every flame of passion, chaste or carnal, would still burn in the absolute unquenched and unabridged, a note absorbed in the harmony of its higher bliss."

(b) But how do all the appearances remain and are absorbed in the Absolute?

> "Fully to realize the existence of the Absolute is for finite beings impossible. In order thus to know we should have to be, and then we should not exist."

Hence, Bradley like Wittegenstein and Paul Tillich realises that in talking about the Absolute, we have to transcend our finitude and the world. Does this position of Bradley differ from that of Shankara? But Bradley's position is that Reality is an all-inclusive and all-harmonious sentient whole. Will not differences within this whole infect it with tension and conflict? Bradley ends his stand paradoxically.

> 'The Absolute has no history of its own, though it contains histories without number?'

Then, he poses a dilemma:

> "If Reality is related to appearances, then they are adjectival to Reality and Reality becomes itself a changing appearance; if Reality does not own appearances, then, Reality becomes qualityless and void."

Shankara rejects the former and accepts the latter, but Bradley remains in an impasse.

2. Again, according to Bradley, all appearances, our truths and errors are *somehow* retained and yet transcended in the Absolute. Does this not mean that the empirical world remains inexplicable in relation to Reality? Hence, the doctrine of māyā is more straightforward and clear even when it has its own difficulties. But like Bradley one does not have to use words and yet eat them up. For Bradley, Truth, Beauty and Goodness remain in the Absolute when their distinctive differences disappear. How is it an improvement on the mergence-doctrine of Shankara?

C. Paul Tillich appears to have profited from the insight of Shankara.

1. Like Shankara, Paul Tillich asserts that reality is Being-itself. This Being is beyond the safety of words, Church and theology. It is 'God above God' i.e., in the language of Shankara, beyond Īshvara.
2. Being-itself upholds all things. Hence any finite segment in the form of symbols can participate, represent and point to Being-itself. It is an improvement on the doctrine of *analogia entis* inasmuch as the unconditioned Transcendent is said to underlie and sustain even the finite segment serving as a symbol. However, working under the influence of *analogia entis*, he thinks that the superlatives in relation to Being-itself becomes diminutives. Hence, like Shankara, Tillich holds that even the highest symbol of God ultimately must be denied in favour of 'God above God', which is the same thing as the 'Brahman' of Shankara.
3. No doubt each symbol in turn comes to be denied, because each symbol is infected with the spirit of self-transcendence on account of its ambiguities within it. But there is no known principle of gradation of the symbols. Here the teaching of the *Gītā*, Gauḍapāda and Shankara is an improvement over Tillich. It is pointed out that *tamas*, *rajas*, *sattva* decide the hierarchical order, both of the worshippers and their respective deities. Again, the meditation on *AUM* determines the nature of successive ascent towards differenceless Brahman. Here there is also the danger of backsliding. Hence, constant endeavour and vigilance is the price of spiritual struggle.
4. Shankara not only gives a rationale of the hierarchical order of deities, but also submits a technique of spiritual progress. The most emphasized technique is of *śramaṇa-manana*, which means the discipline of body, mind and morality. There is the other technique of theisttc worship in the form of *AUM sādhanā*, specially mentioned by Gauḍapāda. However, Shankara knowing that theism is not only illusory, but is likely to be used for purposes other than Brahma-realisation he did not emphasize it as a means of Brahma-realisation. However, Shankara fully used it in relation to *krama-mukti* i.e., liberation through successive stages.

Hence, the technique of Shankara for Brahma-realisation is quite exhaustive and satisfactory.

D. Wittgenstein was essentially a philosopher who sought to know the nature of reality through the analysis of language. But he was not hostile to religion.

1. Any attempt to know God, for Wittgenstein meant going beyond what can be said. It is a region where all religious dialogues end in silence. Any talk about God would trivialize Him. But his doctrine of silence, did not mean nihilism.
2. 'Silence' is the necessary consequence of finding meaning of the world. The solution of the riddle of life in space and time lies outside space and time (*Tractatus* 6.41; 6.4312, 6.432).
3. God is something which shows itself in our talk about God and one is invited to enjoy Him in His being exhibited or shown.
4. Picture-theory about God is important, for it shows the possibility of refining and chiselling the picture by mutual dialogue of the religionists with the end of seeing God of Tillich which means respectful silence. Only in this light the protestant principle of Tillich and *neti, neti* of Shankara can be interpreted.

E. The problem for Advaitism at present is: how to modernise it, how to take social, cultural changes and technology seriously? Moderners realise that the world is a vale of soul-making. But how to use the world in conformity with Advaitism? Ramakrishna Ashrama has adopted a social programme, but is it consistent with Advaitism?

Bibliography

Barth, A., *The Religions of India*, New Delhi, 1969.

Basham, A.L., *The Wonder That was India*, London, 1967.

Belvalkar, S.K. and Ranade, R.D., *History of Indian Philosophy: The Creative Period*, New Delhi, 1974.

Bhandarkar, D.R., *Some Aspects of Ancient Indian Culture*, Madras, 1940.

Bhattacharya, K.D., *A Modern Understanding of Advaita*, Ahmedabad, 1975.

Braithwaite, R.B., *An Empiricist's View of the Nature of Religion*, Cambridge, 1955.

Cave, S., *Redemption: Hindu and Christian*, Milford, 1919.

———, *Christianity and Some Living Religions of the East*, London, 1929.

Dahlquist, Allan, *Megasthenes and Indian Religion*, Delhi, 1977.

Dasgupta, S.N., *A History of Indian Philosophy*, 5 vols., Cambridge, 1952.

Datta, D.M., *Six Ways of Knowing*, London, 1932.

Deussen, Paul, *The System of the Vedanta*, Chicago, 1912.

Farquhar, J.N., *The Crown of Hinduism*, London, 1913, reprinted, New Delhi, 1971.

———, *Modern Religious Movement in India*, London, 1915, reprinted, New Delhi, 1977.

Flew, A. and Macintyre, A., *New Essays in Philosophical Theology*, London, 1958.

Grierson, George, 'Bhakti', *ERE*, 1909.

Griswold, H.D., *The Religion of the Ṛgveda*, reprinted, Delhi, 1923.

Griffith, R.T., *The Hymns of the Ṛgveda*, Delhi, 1976.

Hook, S., *Religious Experience and Truth*, New York, 1961.

Hopkins, W.E., *The Religions of India*, reprinted, New Delhi, 1977.

Hudson, Donald W., *Wittgenstein and Religious Belief*, London, 1975.

Hume, David, *Dialogue Concerning Natural Religion*, London, 1963.
Hume, R.E., *The Thirteen Principal Upanishads*, New Delhi, 1984.
Ikeda, Daisaku, *Buddhism*, Eng. tr. B. Vatson, Amsterdam.
Iyer, M.K.V., *Advaita Vedanta*, Bombay, 1964.
Jha, G., *Shankara Vedanta*, Allahabad, 1939.
Kattackal, J., *Religion and Ethics in Advaita*, Kottayam, 1982.
Mahadevan, T.M.P., *The Philosophy of Advaita*, New Delhi, 1976.
———, *Gauḍapada*, Madras, 1952.
———, *The Hymns of Śaṅkara*, New Delhi, 1986.
Majumdar, R.C., *The History and Culture of the Indian People*, vols. I, XI, Bombay, 1960.
McCrindle, J.W., *Ancient India*, Amsterdam, 1971.
———, *Ancient India as Described by Megasthenes and Arrian*, Calcutta, 1960.
Murty, K. Satchidananda, *Revelation and Reason in Advaita Vedānta*, Delhi, 1974.
Nag, Kalidas, *Greater India*, Bombay, 1960.
Padmapada, *Pancapādika*, no. 197, Baroda, 1948.
Pears, D., *Wittgenstein*, London, 1971.
Pitcher, G., *The Philosophy of Wittgenstein*, Princeton, 1965.
Potter, Karl H., *The Encyclopaedia of Indian Philosophy*, vol. III, *Advaita Vedanta up to Samkara and His Pupils*, part I, Delhi, 1981.
Radhakrishnan, S., *Indian Philosophy*, 2 vols., London, 1951.
Raychaudhuri, Hemachandra, *Materials for the Study of the Early History of the Vaisnava Sect*, New Delhi, 1975.
Rawlinson, H.G., *Intercourse between India and the Western World*, Cambridge, 1916.
Saraswati, Madhusudan, *Advaitasiddhi*, Baroda, 1933.
Sastri, Suryanarayana, *The Bhāmatī Catus-sutri*, Eng. tr., Madras, 1933.
Scott, E.F., 'Gnosticism, Mysticism and Essenes', *ERE*, 1913.
Shankaracarya, *Bhagavadgīta-bhāsya*, Eng. tr. by A. Mahadeva Shastri, Madras, 1918.
Shantaraksita, *Tattvasmgraha*, Baroda, 1926.
Shantinath, Sadhu, *Mayavada*, Poona, 1938.
Sharma, Ramamurti, *Advaita Vedanta*, New Delhi.
Telang, K.T., *The Bhagavadgita*, Delhi, 1964.
Thibaut, George, *Vedānta-Sūtras*, with the commentary of Śaṅkarācārya, parts I-II, Delhi, 1964.
Tillich, Paul, *Systematic Theology*, Chicago.

———, *The Courage To Be*, London, 1963.

Vyas, Ramnarayan, *The Bhagavata Bhakti Cult*, Calcutta, 1977.

Westropp, H.M. and Wake, C. Stanliland, *Ancient Symbol Workship*, London, 1972.

Wilson, H.H., *Religion of the Hindus*, London, 1862.

Journals

Abbott, J.E., 'Bhagavata Purana and the Bhagavadgita', *Indian Antiquary*, 1892.

Bhandarkar, D.R., 'The Origin of the Bhakti-school', *Indian Antiquary*, 1912.

Grierson, George, A. *et al.*, 'Modern Hinduism and Its Debt to the Nestorians', *JRAS*, 1907.

———'Narayaniya and the Bhagavatas', *Indian Antiquary*, 1908.

Jones, W., 'Pythagoras and the Doctrine of Transmigration', *JRAS*, 1909.

Kennedy, J., 'Buddhist Gnosticism: The System of Basilides', *JRAS*, 1902.

———'Krishna, Christianity and Gurjars', *JRAS*, 1907.

Lorinser, 'Traces in the Bhagavadgita of Christian Writings and Ideas', *Indian Antiquary*, 1969.

Weber, A., 'On the Kṛṣṇajanmasthami', *Indian Antiquary*, vol. III.

Index

A Priori 2-5, 45
and Christianity 4-5
and Hinduism 2-4
Religion 2-5, 18, 19-30
Ābhāsavāda 75, 76, 77, 111
Adhyāsa 77, 78
Ahaṁkāra 72
Ajātivāda 70
Ajñāna (Nescience) 63, 77, 78, 80-84, 131
Ālayavijñāna 81
Alexander, S. 1, 22, 34n, 100, 120
Ālvārs 9, 18, 56
Analogia Entis 37-39, 130, 155
Anselm of Canterbury 5, 93
Antaḥkaraṇa 72, 73, 74, 76
Aquinas, St. Thomas 37, 39, 130
Archelaus 14
Aśvaghoṣa 13
Atheism and Religion 29-30
Augustine, St. 4
Avacchedavāda 75, 77
Avidya 71, 73, 77, 78, 79, 82, 84-85, 88
Ayer, A.J. 31, 32, 52, 58, 150

Barth, A. 8, 8n, 9, 13n
Basilides 16
Belvalkar and Ranade 66n, 67n
B.G. Bhagavadgītā
B.G.B. Bhagavadgīta-bhāṣya
Bhāgavatas 112
Bhāgavat Purāṇa 7, 7n
Bhaktamālā 6, 9, 14
Bhakti 6, 9, 9n, 10, 89
Origin of 6, 7
Bhāmatī 68n, 88n, 91n, 106n, 121
B-Jñāna (*Brahma-jñāna*) 92, 93

Bonhoeffer, D. 24
Bradley, F.H. 53, 131, 153, 154
Brahman and Īshvara 88-92, 111
Brahman and Jīva 74-77
Braithwaite, R.B. 60, 143, 149, 149n
Buddha and Christ 13-14
Buddhism and Christianity 1-16

Caste 139, 140, 141, 142
Causality
Asatkāryavāda 64
Pariṇāmavāda 65
Satkāryavāda 65
Vivartavāda 65, 94
Chattopadhyaya, Debi Prasād 121
Christianity 4
and Hinduism 5-11
Clement of Alexandria 4, 11, 12, 15, 17
Confession (*Aposatha*) 12
Copleston, F.C. 32, 38n

Dahlquist, Allan 10n
Dasgupta, S. 82, 82n, 90, 90n, 111, 111n
Deussen, Paul 71n, 82, 82n, 9, 90n, 111, 111n
Dīkṣita, Appaya 110

Essene 12, 13, 13n
EW (Empirical World)

Findlay, J.N. 24, 31, 52, 146, 146n
First Cause 57-58
Flew, A.G.N. 25, 31, 32, 52, 58, 147-48
Freud, S. 22, 23n, 132
Fromm, Erich 23

Gauḍapāda 53, 62, 77, 79, 98, 99, 114, 115, 126, 133, 135, 155
Gnosticism 12, 15, 15n, 16, 17
Gnosis 130, 131
God 86-87
  above or beyond God 53, 63, 130, 155
Godot 28
Grierson, George A. 6, 6n, 7, 7n, 9, 10, 14n
Griswold, H. 78

Hanumānanāṭaka (*Mahānāṭaka*) 2
Hare, R.M. 60, 148f
Heiler, F. 5, 5n
Hick, J. 25, 32
Hinduism and Christianity 11-19
Hook, S. 41n, 42
Hopkins, E.W. 6, 11
Hudson, W. Donald 33, 33n, 52, 55, 55n, 58, 59n, 61n, 62
Hume, David 97, 97n
Hume, R.E. 64n

Irwin, John 13
Īshvara and Brahman 88-92, 111
Īshvara and Māyā 89
Iyer, M.K.V. 86n, 100, 100n, 111n

Jacob, A. 125, 128
Jerome, St. 12, 14
Jha, G. 106n, 107n, 110, 110n
Jīvanmukti 101, 125, 126, 127, 128n, 129
Jñāna 15, 101, 104, 107, 116
Jñāna-Karma-Samuccayavāda 102, 107, 108, 142
Josaphat (St) 14
Jung, C.G. 23, 51, 63, 134
  and Individuation 27-28

Kant, I. 27, 31, 36, 45, 49, 68, 96n, 103, 106n, 132, 146, 148, 150
Karma
  Naimittika 102
  Niṣiddha 102
  Nitya 102
Karmakāṇḍa
  Instrumental Value of 106n, 107
  liberation and 100-8
Karma-Sannyāsa 100, 101, 142
Kattackal, J. 124n
Keith, A.B. 7, 9, 11
Kennedy, J. 7, 8n, 9, 15, 16, 16n
Khair, G.S. 11
Khushwant Singh 29-30
Knowledge
  by Acquaintance 34, 100, 119
  by Contemplation 100, 120
  by Description 119
Köhler, W. 101
Kṛṣṇaism 6, 7, 8, 10
Kṛṣṇajanmāṣṭamī 5
Kusumāñjali 3

Liberation (*mokṣa*) 98-100
  and *Jñānakāṇḍa* 115-18
  and *Karmakāṇḍa* 100-08
  and Worship 108-13
Lorinser, 6, 6n

Madonna and Child 7-8
Mahadevan, T.M.P. 72, 173
Mahānāṭaka 2
Mahāvākya 56, 65, 131
  and *Brahma-jñāna* 102, 115, 116, 118, 121, 122-24
Mainkar, T.G. 79n
Manichaenism 12
Masih, Y. 2n, 148
Māyā 77-80, 86, 87, 89
  and *Avidya* 77ff
Megasthenes, 10, 10n
Mishra, Maṇḍana 88, 103, 107, 110n, 112, 123, 127, 128, 129, 151
Mishra, Vācaspati 88, 97, 123
Mukti 101, 102
  Karma 102, 112, 113
Murty, K S. 118n

Nag, Kalidas 14n
Nāgārjuna 33, 53, 58, 59, 100, 137, 142-43
Nāgasena 33, 58, 137
Naiṣkarmyasiddhi 107n, 124n, 125n, 128, 129
Nakamura, H. 3n

Nestorians 6, 7
Nicholas of Cusa 5
Niṣkāma Karma 132, 133

Om (*a*, *u*, *m*) 114-15, 133, 140
  a (*Viśva*) 114
  u (*Prājña*) 114
Ontological theory of *a priori* 19-22
  of *Atman* 93-94

Padmapāda 91, 96, 105, 124
Pañcapādikā 92, 96, 105
Panikkar, K.M. 17
Pāṇini 10
Patañjali 10
Pears, David 62, 62n
Phaedo 19
Phaedrus 19
Philo of Alexandria 4, 12
Pitcher, George 119n
Popper, Karl R. 57, 57n, 147
Potter, K.H. 68n, 74n, 84n, 101n, 102n, 104n, 105n, 107n, 108n, 110n, 125n
Prasaṅkhyāna 107, 123, 123n, 124
Pratibimbavāda 75, 76, 77
Price, H.H. 54
Pythagoras, 13, 16, 17, 18

Radhakrishnan, S. 3, 4n, 141
Ramakrishna 112, 156
Rāmānuja 7, 18, 19, 29, 36, 89, 121, 131, 132
Ramsey, Ian 120
Ranade, R.D. 79n
Rawlinson, H.G. 8, 8n, 9, 12, 12n, 13n, 14n, 17, 18n
Robinson, (Bishop) 24
Russell, B. 30, 31, 53, 100, 118, 150

Saṃvṛti
  Mithyā 80
  Tathya 80
Sāṅkṛtyāyana, Rāhula 139n
Saraswati, Madhusudana 68, 72
Sarvamukti 129, 141
Sat 66
Scott, E.J. 15n
Secularism 129
Shankara 33, 48, 53, 58, 59, 61, 62, 63
  and theism 86-92
  and theistic proofs 90
Sharma, Ramamurti 78
Shudra 9
Subramaniam, K.R. 9, 10n
Sureshvara 107, 108, 121, 124, 129

Tajjalān 116
Tat Tvam Asi 122, 123, 124
Telang, K.T. 11
Thomas, St. Aquinas 111-13
Tillich, Paul 17, 20-22, 20n, 21n, 34, 39-52, 40n, 41n, 49n, 55, 58, 59, 61, 62, 63, 130, 135, 136, 138, 140, 143 144, 150, 154f
Transmigration 15, 16, 19
  Indian 15
  Pythagorean 15
Turiya 82, 114, 126, 131
Turner, J.E. 11

Udayanācārya 3
Uposatha (rite of confession) 12

Vaiṣṇava 12
Vasudevism 10, 11, 12, 112
Vivekakhyāti 101
Vivekananda 112

Waismann, F. 54
Weber, A. 6, 6n
Wisdom, John 44, 52, 146, 146n
Wittgenstein, L. 33, 34, 37, 52 61, 62, 94n, 119, 120, 131, 135, 136, 140, 143, 144, 154f, 156
Wordsworth, W. 1